D. H. LAWRENCE: THE CROYDON YEARS

D. H. Lawrence (c. 1908)

D. H. LAWRENCE, THE CROYDON YEARS

By Helen Corke

Introduction by Warren Roberts

UNIVERSITY OF TEXAS PRESS · AUSTIN

INTRODUCTION

Many people who knew D. H. Lawrence have written about him, but none has done so with more perception or less ostentation than Helen Corke, whose *Lawrence & APOCALYPSE* appeared in 1933. Her book is unobtrusive, but she knew Lawrence and she knew what Lawrence was about.

A teacher herself, she was intimately interested in Lawrence's work both as teacher and writer. He gave her his first novel, *The White Peacock,* to read in manuscript, and she was the heroine of his second novel, *The Trespasser,* which Lawrence wrote from her record of a personal tragedy paralleling that of Helena in the novel.

Curiously enough, it was *Sons and Lovers,* with which the name of Helen Corke is not usually associated, that marked the turning point in their relationship. The reading of *The White Peacock* gave Helen Corke an introduction to Eastwood, the Haggs Farm, and Lawrence's friends there, including Jessie Chambers, the original of Emily in the first novel and of Miriam in the later *Sons and Lovers.* The warm and vivid friendship which developed between the two women after their actual introduction by Lawrence was based upon their common interest in him as poet and genius; the effect upon Jessie of Lawrence's portrait of her in *Sons and Lovers* contributed directly to a break in this bond. From the time of the book's publication Jessie imagined that she wanted to forget Lawrence, and the presence, the very being of Helen was an unwelcome reminder. Helen her-

self regarded the Miriam portrait as unjustifiable, and was re-
pelled by Lawrence's declaration to Jessie, "With 'should' and
'ought' I have nothing to do."

The four documents reprinted in this volume constitute Helen
Corke's major comment on Lawrence the man and Lawrence the
artist. Her record is significant because she alone of Lawrence's
friends was in a position to view him objectively during the most
critical period of his life. The years at Croydon were for Lawrence
a time of crisis, during which he matured as an individual and as
an artist. Helen Corke was closely involved with him in the personal relationships which culminated in his first major work,
Sons and Lovers. It was the completion of this novel which
marked Lawrence's final break with his Nottinghamshire background, when his long association with Jessie Chambers ended,
and his meeting with Frieda at Easter, 1912, changed the course
of his life.

"Portrait of D. H. Lawrence: 1909–1910" first appeared in
The Texas Quarterly for Spring, 1962; it is an excerpt from Miss
Corke's unpublished autobiography, "Not in Entire Forgetfulness," which documents the period of her friendship with Lawrence in Croydon. This portion of the autobiography covers the
first revision of *The White Peacock* and the writing of *The Trespasser,* the novel with which Miss Corke was most intimately
concerned.

"D. H. Lawrence's Princess" is a memoir of Jessie Chambers
published originally in a limited edition by the Merle Press
at Thames Ditton, Surrey. This reminiscence is concerned primarily with Helen Corke's sensitive and sympathetic involvement
in Jessie Chambers' tragic relationship with Lawrence. The moving account of Helen Corke's last meeting with Jessie Chambers
in Nottingham, ten years after Lawrence's death, is a poignant
epilogue to the story of Miriam and Paul in *Sons and Lovers.*

The short essay "Concerning *The White Peacock*" is a critical discussion of Lawrence's first novel. It was written after his death when the manuscript of the novel, originally known as "Nethermere," was discovered by Helen Corke, "forgotten, on the shelf of a lumber cupboard," in her old home.

Students will always be grateful for Helen Corke's reminiscences of Lawrence's novel *The White Peacock* and for her account of his years in Croydon, but her basic judgment on Lawrence is found in *Lawrence & APOCALYPSE*, where her sense of history and her understanding of Lawrence succeeded in preserving, as one reviewer wrote at the time, "an attitude of critical sympathy in writing of Lawrence that in a majority of books about him and his writings is conspicuously absent." More than this, Helen Corke drew with unerring precision from the text of *Apocalypse* the gist of Lawrence's teaching about the nature of man. She realized the importance of his belief in the positive value of life, so eloquently affirmed in *Apocalypse*:

For man the vast marvel is to be alive. For man, as for flower and beast and bird, the supreme triumph is to be most vividly, most perfectly alive. Whatever the unborn and the dead may know, they cannot know the beauty, the marvel of being alive in the flesh.

This was the text of the young Lawrence's teaching to Helen Corke, and it remained with her, unforgotten, through a long life.

WARREN ROBERTS

Austin

PREFACE

No communication of any kind had passed between D. H. Lawrence and myself from the year 1913 to that of his death. Absorbed in a busy life of teaching and writing, I relegated my memories of the Croydon days to a remote background. My outlook on life became almost blatantly objective.

The realisation of Lawrence's death caused a sharp reaction. The compulsion of his vivid personality returned, and with it the charged atmosphere of the 1908–1912 period. The colours of the immediate present faded as the intensity of the earlier experience reasserted itself. Once again I lived with my memories.

An Orioli proof of Lawrence's last book came into my hands. From the pages of *Apocalypse* the young, questing spirit of twenty years past saluted me. What did I think of his new study? A discussion developed, and *Lawrence &* APOCALYPSE was written at speed during the autumn of 1932. If Lawrence leaned by my shoulder during its writing, the quiet figure of John of Patmos was also present in the near background. The book was published by Wm. Heinemann in the spring of 1933. After the war no copies remained; the edition had shared the fate of the majority of unsold books in Britain—to supply a shortage of paper for current printing it had been sent to the pulping mills.

Six years after the passing of Jessie Chambers I was approached by Mr. Stanley Mercer, of the Merle Press, Thames Ditton, for an essay relating to my memory of Lawrence which might be suitably included in a series of short biographies to be issued in a *de luxe* limited edition, each copy numbered and signed. Jessie's letters to me, written during the period of her breakaway from Lawrence, had lain by in a drawer since 1912. They were poignant, beautifully expressed, and unquestionably sincere. With little help from me they would present the woman's side of the Paul and Miriam story. The writing of *A Memory of Jessie Chambers* became an act of justice to an intimate friend.

The whole of the small edition (200 copies only) has long since found its rest on the shelves of reference libraries and collectors of rare books, and it seems timely that the *Memory* should be revived again in the present volume.

After the final correction of proofs for Lawrence's first novel, *The White Peacock,* the author had given the manuscript to me. The brown-paper parcel, tied with string, lay by for twenty years. In September, 1930, I untied the string and looked again at the familiar handwriting; then I turned to the first-edition copy, also Lawrence's gift, and read with a new and absorbed attention the half-forgotten story. The sequence was the writing of the essay *Concerning the White Peacock.* It appears to have been offered, as soon as finished, to a London journal called *Everyman,* which declined it, and I have no record of any further attempt to publish it in England.

The interest taken in my Lawrence memories by the editors of *The Texas Quarterly* resulted in that journal's publication, in November, 1962, of the extract from my unpublished autobiography which here appears as *Portrait of D. H. Lawrence 1909– 1910.* The autobiography was begun in 1939, dropped during the war, and subsequently finished in 1961. The manuscript is now in the possession of the Humanities Research Center of the University of Texas. It is in two parts, entitled respectively "Not in Entire Forgetfulness" and "The Light of Common Day."

H. C.

ACKNOWLEDGMENTS

I would sincerely thank A. S. Frere, O.B.E. Chairman of Wm. Heinemann, Ltd., for his gift to me in 1932, of a fine prepublication copy of Lawrence's *Apocalypse*, which he had received from Orioli of Florence, the original publisher. The inspiration to write my commentary, *Lawrence &* APOCALYPSE arose from the reading of this admirable proof.

My thanks are due also to Mr. Stanley Mercer, of the Merle Press, Thames Ditton, England, for the suggestion which resulted in the writing of *Lawrence's Princess: A Memory of Jessie Chambers,* and for the beauty and clarity of the little book's presentation.

For permission to quote extensively from Jessie Chambers' *Letters,* and to use the portrait of her included with this book's illustrations, my grateful thanks go to Dr. J. D. Chambers and the other executors of Jessie's estate.

For the use of certain short quotations from the works of Swinburne, John Davidson, and Gilbert Murray, and for an extract from one of Lawrence's letters to me, I acknowledge my debt to the executors and publishers concerned.

Finally, *D. H. Lawrence: The Croydon Years* owes its publication to the interest and initiative of my most kind and sympathetic friend Warren Roberts. I hope that he will accept my warmest thanks for the encouragement and help he has given me during the book's preparation, and that its inclusion in the list of the University of Texas Press may be a lasting satisfaction to him and to the Press.

H. C.

CONTENTS

ILLUSTRATIONS

PORTRAIT OF

D. H. LAWRENCE

1909–1910

(from *The Texas Quarterly*, V,
No. 1 [Spring, 1962], 168–177)

PRESENTLY AGNES BRINGS David Lawrence with her when she makes her evening appearance. He sits down in a fireside chair, his head thrown back, arms hanging over those of the chair, legs stretched across the hearthrug, while Agnes and I play Mozart or Beethoven sonatas. The playing is very unsatisfying—Agnes's loud, hard *fortes* and meaningless phrasing, my tonelessness. When the sonatas are finished, we talk desultorily—or Agnes and David talk, and I am silent. It is Agnes who will go into the kitchen to fetch coffee; and then the young man suddenly brings a book from his pocket, with "Listen! Will you hear this?" Half a dozen lines from a poem. "What do you think of it—shall we go on?" Or he may hand me without speaking a small, thick notebook, and indicate a written poem on the open page. There is always something arresting about these manuscript poems, something which lifts for the moment the weight of my inertia, jerks the sullen setting of my brooding thought from its concentration upon memories. I am aroused to discussion; even, after the two have departed, to reflection on what has been said.

David Lawrence is not without place in those absorbing memories. He had entered during the anticipatory springtime, that day on the Heath, and I had mentioned him to H. B. M., calling him *Wunderkind.*

Now in the autumn, he returns, with no less delicate a perception of the autumn in my heart. I am at first aware of his unobtrusive sympathy, then of a tentative endeavour to reawaken my

interest in literature and art, not as mere subjects, but in their relation to personal experience. D. H. L. will lure me from the isle
of memory with the quiet voice of the summer sea itself.

> In Salamis, filled with the foaming of
>   billows, and murmur of bees,
> Old Telamon stayed from his roaming, long ago,
>   on a throne of the seas;
> Looking out on the hills, olive-laden, enchanted,
>   where first from the earth
> The grey-gleaming fruit of the maiden Athena
>   had birth.[1]

Voice and rhythm enter into the pattern of my dream—that
dream of an island wherein I saw romance and reality as not two
eternals, but one eternal. It is as if on the mist curtain enclosing
that island I see the forms of the Greeks, and hear, mingled with
the sound of the waves on its beaches, the tragic chorus of Euripides. Through Gilbert Murray, through Lawrence, the spirit of
irony and pity inspiring Euripides brings the classic tragedy of
the Troades into touch with the individual tragedy, and they are
woven together into the mind-stuff of my life. D. H. L. begins
with the chorus themes; then he ventures: "Will you hear the
whole?"—and I lie hour-long in my chair on the opposite side of
the hearth, watching the fire flicker and glow, seeing it now and
again redden Lawrence's high forehead, the thick, straight,
goldenish hair above, the fair, bushy eyebrows over the deep-set,
blue-grey eyes, the straight nose and oval curve of the cheek.

From the "letter" to H. B. M. Oct. 20th:

I am going to try and do a little German with the help of D. H. L.,
so that I may get more insight into Wagner's philosophy. . . . I used
to find D. H. L.'s company stimulating—he is so eager for experience,

---

[1] Euripides, *The Trojan Women*, Trans. Gilbert Murray (London,
Allen & Unwin, 1905).

so self-confident and clear-headed, so fearless in criticism. He holds the cup of life before him and contemplates it with great satisfaction— he is going to drain it before putting it down. He stimulates me to greater misery now—I who stand holding a broken cup.

The German lessons begin with a little ragged copy of German lyric verse, bought for twopence from a secondhand bookstall. This verse, Lawrence points out, is very simple in form; I can memorise a poem easily, and become familiar with the phrasing before coming to the grind of grammar books. So I approach Goethe and Heine directly:

> Über allen Gipfeln
> ist Ruh;
> In allen Wipfeln
> spürest du
> Kaum einen Hauch;
> Die Vögelein schweigen im Walde,
> Warte nur—balde,
> ruhest du auch.

The weariness that haunts these poems, the cry of the German mind for "rest," is all in accordance with my mood. Self-indulgently I will linger over the chords that accompany Siegfried's parting words to the broken Wotan, "Ruh, ruh, du Gott." Or pick out from the *Valkyrie* score the lovely interlude expressing Siegmund's watch over the sleeping Sieglinde. But there is a more vigorous note struck in Heine's *Thalatta:* "Sei mir gegrüsst, du ewiges Meer." It awakens older echoes.

Lawrence brings me also at this time the poems of John Davidson, who, totally unfitted for life in a commercialised world, has recently drowned himself off the Cornish coast. One of his poems I think I can pass on to my children—they learn it readily:

> The boat is chafing at our long delay,
> and we must leave too soon
> the spicy sea-pinks and the inborne spray—

the tawny sands, the moon—
Keep us, O Thetis, in our western flight,
watch from thy pearly throne
our vessel, speeding onwards into night,
to reach a land unknown.

My mother encourages Lawrence's visits. For her he has always
a gay raillery, tinged with deference, and with a sympathetic un-
dertone. I fancy she sees in him the suggestion of a grown son
Frank. My father shows a nervous avoidance of him, and puts up
a defence of light sarcasm if the younger man attempts to engage
him in any serious discussion.

David Lawrence has always a cough. In February I hear that influenza is keeping him from school. On a Saturday afternoon I
call at his lodging. He is still in bed, but better. He asks me to
bring him a thick brown paper parcel which is standing on the
floor in a corner of the room; he unpacks it and shows me the
manuscript of a novel with the title "Nethermere." He says it is
his first novel and has been accepted by the firm of Heinemann,
who return it for a final revision. Will I read the manuscript and
make suggestions, especially marking passages showing prolixity?
As I read the close, cursive, legible script, my mind is again
lifted from its chosen absorption, and sent on two excursions, one
into the days of childhood and early adolescence, when author-
ship was my ideal and goal, the other into a new country, the
Midlands, to see Lawrence, the observant wanderer, the impersonal, almost bodiless intelligence, moving among a little crowd
of country folk. The raw February day marks a stage in our relationship. Hitherto Lawrence has been content to minister to my
needs, and I to accept his ministrations. This day sees his first request of me, his first demand on my activity. We enter a stage of
mutual cooperation which brings us together more frequently.
The German verse, the long discussions relative to the revision of

the novel and to the other books he brings for my reading, may occupy three evenings a week. From "Nethermere" I get incidental pictures of his home life, but make no effort to coordinate them.

D. H. L. sees me put away a writing pad when he enters and presently asks what I am writing. It is only the long letter which there seems no need to end. I have finished a brief diary of the Island experience. He asks if he may see a scrap of my work. There is, I tell him, no "work." But the claim his intuitional sympathy has established is strengthened by the coincidence of his presence upon the Island during that first week of last August— and my experience is already undergoing in my mind the first of the modifications whereby the raw material of events is shaped into works of art. I give him the Freshwater diary. There is a new urgency in his voice when he returns it. "What are you going to *do* with these prose poems?" he asks. I reply, nothing. They are written; it is enough. He declares, and insists, that the act of expression in writing preassumes a reader, and also that human experience is the common property of humanity. I only know that my impulse was to use the medium of rhythmic prose to embalm what I had found beautiful. I am glad that the writing is good enough to appeal to D. H. L.

He returns to the subject later—comes with the request that he take the diary and expand its theme—use the poems as basis for a more comprehensive rendering of the story. He will bring me his work as it grows; nothing shall stand with which I am not in agreement. It will be a finished study, based upon my fertile suggestions. He is very eager. I think of the music H. B. M. should have lived to write, and assent. Indubitably Lawrence is a poet. The power of seizing upon subtle analogies, of perceiving delicate relationships, of apprehending old and new rhythms, of capturing truth in symbols, is his in very great measure. There is an element

of wonder in my contemplation of him, and in the coincidence of
his appearance at just this juncture of my life.

One evening this spring D. H. L. brings me the first chapters of
"The Saga of Siegmund," saying that there is the beginning of a
work of art that must be a saga since it cannot be a symphony. He
asks me to scrutinise it in detail, as I have done the manuscript of
Nethermere. I refuse; my part in this book is that of guide.
David must see and feel very clearly what he has to write. He
must know H. B. M. as I know him. It is the one thing I would
do—realise H. B. M. for David Lawrence. Life finds a purpose.
The closing words of the Chorus in the *Alcestis* of Euripides become charged with an almost personal significance:

> There be many shapes of mystery;
> and many things God brings to be,
> past hope or fear,
> and the end men looked for cometh not,
> and a path is there where no man thought.
> So hath it fallen here.[2]

At weekends this spring Lawrence and I ramble over the Surrey
downs, pondering and probing at the three major mysteries of
existence, life, love, and death. The presence of H. B. M. seems
never far away. Each Saturday morning we meet—at Purley or
Addiscombe or Penge—all jumping-off places for the open country. D. H. L. knows the flora of the lanes better than I, and our
talk is often mixed with incidental study of botany. I have a sense
of peace, a detached kind of happiness; he is serious and whim-
sical by turns. Once, in a lane, we pass a fallen elm tree, probably
blown down during an autumn gale, but not utterly uprooted—a
small thicket of bright green shoots is rising from its horizontal
trunk. Perhaps my life is to be like that of the elm tree.

[2] Trans. Gilbert Murray.

Lawrence does most of his writing at night—much too late at night. Self-absorbed, I do not notice how much the work is taxing his nerves—the night work added to a wearing, noisy day at school. He tells me once that he writes half drunk, but this I discount as a touch of the pose which, evident a year ago, has almost disappeared. He brings the manuscript to me, chapter by chapter, as written. The intuition it shows, the tense concentration, the rare symbolism, fill me with wonder. My regard for David Lawrence begins to be touched with awe. Again romance and realism join hands.

He reads aloud to me the *Ave Atque Vale* of Swinburne—reads it as if it were a ritual elegy for H. B. M.

> Shall I strew on thee rose, or rue, or laurel,
> Brother, on this that is the dust of thee—
> Or quiet sea-flower, moulded by the sea—?
>
> .   .   .
>
> Not thee—O never thee, in all Time's changes,
> Not thee, but this, the sound of thy sad soul,
> The shadow of thy swift spirit—this shut scroll
> I lay my hand on, and not death estranges
> My spirit from communion with thy song
> Is it well now, where love can do no wrong?
>
> .   .   .
>
> O sleepless heart and sombre soul unsleeping
> That were athirst for death, and no more life
> And no more love—for peace and no more strife!

It is to me an opiate, this verse. I wake suddenly on a day when David and I are wandering in Kentish hill country. At the top of a green hill which falls away to meadow, David challenges me to race down the slope, passes me, and turns in my path, catching me as I try to check. Recovering balance, we laugh, but David clasps me longer than is necessary; when we move he holds my hand fast, protectively and possessively; we are silent.

I try to face the position objectively. It may be that David's feeling for me is quite other than the deep affection I have for him. The thought is disquieting, but I argue that his present reaction is induced by the writing of the Saga. He is putting himself, imaginatively, in H. B. M.'s place; the conditions are both abnormal and temporary. I must not confuse the man with the artist. When this work is finished he will see me from another angle and in other lights.

When the writing of the Saga is finished, Lawrence's mind, released from concentration upon the book's personnel, reverts to a problem of his own. He tells me more about his home, his family, and of a friend—a girl friend with whom he has a special intimacy—the original of Emily in "Nethermere." She is a farmer's daughter, now teaching in a Nottingham school. Their long-standing friendship, hitherto intellectual rather than passional, is discouraged by his mother, who can recognise no bond between man and woman but that of marriage. It seems that the question of marriage is being forced upon them against their will. Lawrence does not want to marry Jessie Chambers; he would rather they remained friends. At first I listen casually, without much interest, to this talk of people who are nothing to me, whom, if I met, I should probably find unendurable. But my own reaction awakens me to the facts of the situation, and to the passing of the phase of isolation induced by Lawrence's absorption in the writing of the Saga. He brings me a short story just written, in which he quotes one of Jessie Chambers' letters to him. The story begins: "Muriel has sent me some mauve primroses." Then and thereafter this friend of Lawrence's is "Muriel" between us.

In July he tells me that Muriel is coming to spend a weekend

with him; he announces this in an offhand and irritated manner.
Do I want to see her? Should I like to meet her? I am not in-
curious; it is arranged that Lawrence shall bring Muriel to Hayes
Common for a Sunday afternoon walk. I set out with misgivings,
even prepared to dislike one whose claim on him is evidently so
strong and subtle—a claim he owns and yet disallows. Will not
this girl resent my presence—shall I not feel an intruder? Each of
us has Lawrence's portrait of the other; she has read the Saga; I
know her as the Emily of "Nethermere."

The afternoon marks another stage in my education. Indubitably Muriel belongs to my world—she may enter it in her own
right. I feel that she brings to it a new element. Light and colour
and movement, joy and anguish that world knows; her presence
ensures it warmth. Not sun heat, or the unreliable blaze of a fire
that scorches or sinks to ash, but a glow that relaxes, comforts, sus-
tains. In retrospect I always see her in a claret red dress—perhaps
it was the colour she wore on that afternoon of our introduction.
She was taller than I, her shoulders a little bent. Dark, silky hair
waved low over her forehead and fell in little curls at her neck
and temples; her face was pale, or suddenly, momentarily flushed.
Her brown eyes, even when she smiled, were sorrowful; they had
a grieved expression as if, impersonally, she were always conscious of the pain of the world. As D. H. L. had noted in "Nethermere," "Some people, instead of bringing with them clouds of
glory, trail clouds of sorrow; they are born with 'the gift of sorrow'—sorrows, they proclaim, alone are real. . . . Sorrow is
beauty, and the supreme blessedness. You read it in their eyes and
in the tones of their voices. Emily had the gift of sorrow."

"It fascinated me, but it drove me to rebellion," comments the
Cyril of the book.

My reaction had nothing in it of rebellion. Muriel, ready to
transmute my sorrow into beauty, even to see me as beautiful on

account of it, drew me at once into her own life, made her vision for a while my own.

We return to Lawrence's lodging to tea. He, in a cynical mood, lies on the hearthrug and reads with slashing criticism a book of modern verse. Immediately after tea I leave. He sees Muriel to the station, and then calls on me, late. What do I think of Muriel? What is he to do in relation to her? And what of ourselves?

I tell him that I think he will ultimately go back to her—how, I wonder, being conscious of the still warmth of her, can he do otherwise! He is cynical and impatient: I feel that his desire at the moment is towards me, and I am glad he loves me. Yet there is no rest, no assurance in this love of David's, because there comes with it an impossible demand. A demand not merely for passion given and returned, but for the absorption of my being in his. I think he knows he is asking the impossible, and beats himself against the knowledge.

My mind is divided between retrospection and the problem of the immediate future. David Lawrence writes to me from his home. The letter is a scrawl of huge, thick characters, in marked contrast to his usual even, slanting hand.

I began to write to you at sunset. Now it is starlight, big scintillating stars; it is nearly midnight. I am as miserable as the devil . . . Muriel met me. She is very pretty and very wistful. She came to see me yesterday. She kisses me. It makes my heart feel like ashes. But then she kisses me more and moves my sex fire. Mein Gott! It is hideous. I have promised to go there tomorrow, to stay till Thursday. If I have courage I shall not stay. It is my present intention not to stay. I must tell her— I must tell her also that we ought finally and definitely to part.—if I have the heart to tell her. . . . I am rather a despicable object. I wish I had not come home. . . . Do not forget me, and do not smile too wearily as you read.[3]

There is a postscript: "The writing is so bad because my mother is waiting for me to go to bed—won't leave me up."

This letter presents with unmistakable clearness an aspect of Lawrence which seems almost to reverse our former relationships. Since last October I have been dependent upon him for force and direction; he has seemed to take upon himself the responsibility of recharging my depleted energy. This weakness of his, this indecision and self-distrust, are distressingly contradictory. Passively I have accepted the fact of his presence at my side all these months, assuming no concern or responsibility on his account. He has lured me back among the living; now I have to begin again to use my own volition, to make decisions, perhaps for him as well as for myself.

Our minds are extraordinarily intimate, and their perceptions reciprocal. Our physical relationship has been that of brother and sister, but since early summer I have become increasingly aware of the demand that he, as instinctive man, makes upon me as woman. I cannot indefinitely ignore it; but there is no instinctive response of my own body. My desire is not towards him. I do not want either to marry him and bear him children, or to be his mistress.

I am now twenty-eight, and in no other sense immature. I think I cannot be "woman" in the ordinary meaning of the term. Apparently I represent a variation in human type. The old, early feeling of "aloneness" remains. Whence came the folk idea of the changeling, the half-human?

[3] Letter from D. H. Lawrence to Helen Corke; copyright © 1962 by Angelo Ravagli and C. Montague Weekley; reprinted by permission of The Viking Press, Inc.

I hate Lawrence's precise classification, "You are not the wife and mother type—you must be *femme de plaisir*." It is not true. It is one of his rare stupidities.

On impulse I write to Muriel, inviting her to spend some days at my home before her holiday ends. She has never seen the sea from the south coast. I will show her the places where the happiest part of my childhood was passed.

We make a day's excursion to Newhaven.

Muriel's presence fills me with peace. It is induced by the low tones of her voice, her reflective manner, and the dark, innate warmth of her. Sometimes she slips into an absent mood, and moves almost like the blind, and then, again, she will seem suddenly happy in being with me, and I hear her laugh, low and full as her voice. Our talk today is all of personal relations, of David, of her old home, the Haggs Farm, the centre of her association with him; and of my childhood with Evelyn by the sea. She draws me, very gently, to talk of H. B. M., and the writing of the Saga. Presently she asks me to tell her, if I can, what David *is* to me. I try to explain, perhaps as much to myself as to Muriel.

How can he be other than infinitely content with her?

The August day is sunny and breezy; we sit in a little hollow of the Downs, sheltered from the wind, and watch the sea foaming in the Bay as we talk. And at night I bring Muriel home, and see with secret satisfaction that my mother and father are both responding to her like pimpernel to the sun—their faces relaxed, their voices full of pleasure.

Some change in my relationship with David is inevitable, I know, when we meet again after the August separation. September makes this more obvious. The grace and tenderness of his former bearing towards me show rarely; he is sullen, or irritation flares suddenly into fierce irony and pitiless criticism. An undiagnosed illness of his mother fills him with foreboding, adding to the depression caused by his indecision over future relations with Muriel and myself.

I lie awake at night thinking miserably of the situation. My sense of responsibility is awakened. It was so easy to admit David into the zone of intimacy between H. B. M. and myself—David the sensitive, impersonal artist. I should have foreseen that he might endanger his impersonality—but grief is stupid, and his nearness, his comprehending sympathy, were healing. The onus of the position is with me—I am senior by more than three years.

If it were merely a sex debt I have incurred, it might be paid. Then, eventually, David and Muriel could marry. *Would* they complement one another—would they be happy? I feel that Muriel believes so, but David, sometimes uncertainly and sometimes emphatically, denies it.

October opens with still, hot weather. At the weekend David and I go to the Sussex Downs and the sea. We descend the cliffs near Rottingdean and walk along the shore to Newhaven—a desolate shingle beach heaped with decaying seaweed. David, walking by my side, is remote, the cynical mood paramount; my companion of the springtime is a memory, insubstantial as those figures of childhood who persist only in the emotional atmosphere wrapping the old town. We pass round the harbour to Seaford, and ask a night's lodging at a large grey cottage near the beach. The season is over; there are no other visitors staying in the cottage. A woman prepares us a meal, and then leaves, after assigning us rooms at either end of a corridor.

I am tired and sleep at once, to wake at dawn with a fearful sense of loneliness and disintegration, as one might wake suddenly in a new world, without memory or foreknowledge. The objects in the room stand stark, black against the dead white of a dawn filtering through fog. There is a muffled beat of surf from the beach, otherwise complete silence. The bark of a dog or the crow of a cock might have assuaged my strange terror—but it increases until it is not to be borne. I run barefoot along the corridor to the door of David's room and stand there listening for a movement. I hear his voice muttering in sleep. Even the half-human sound steadies me. I need not wake him. Returning to my room I dress, and presently close the cottage door softly, to walk by the sea in a vanishing mist of azure and gold. A high, dark-blue tide runs full and foaming up the beach, and my miasma is lost in a turmoil of spray and sunlight. Later, David joins me, the harshness gone from his mood.

I try, not very successfully, to express this experience; Lawrence takes the result, which I have called "Fantasy" and paraphrases it with the objective poem "Coldness in Love."

The proofs of "Nethermere" arrive from the publisher's office for correction. But the editor wants a change of title—says that for an unknown author's first work a more striking one is necessary. It becomes *The White Peacock*, and by that name should be published before Christmas. Lawrence brings round the proofs, and we correct them together, but he seems to have lost all interest in the book. During October he goes home to Eastwood at weekends, and returns with eyes like steel in a set, white face. His mother is dying of cancer. Until now I have not realised how large a part in his life the mother plays. Nor, until a year later, when he is writing "Paul Morel," do I really understand how home influence affected his attitude towards Jessie Chambers.

D. H. LAWRENCE'S
"PRINCESS": A MEMORY
OF JESSIE CHAMBERS

(The Merle Press, Thames Ditton,
Surrey, 1951)

IN THE SPRING of 1910, D. H. Lawrence was revising for publication his first-written novel, "Nethermere," later re-named *The White Peacock*. During many evenings he and I sat in my mother's little green sitting-room, discussing points of the revision. Since childhood, writing had been my preoccupation, but there were no writers in my family, and Lawrence's manuscript was the first, other than my own, that I had seen. It intrigued me greatly.

The story gave me a picture of a Midland valley, and the people living in and around it. I looked again at the young Midlander with the high forehead and deep-set, keen grey eyes, who lounged in the chair by the fire. This valley was David's country; these people were his people. I saw him differently, with a background. Hitherto he had been simply David, a new friend of pronounced individuality, who with persistent but mistaken kindness was trying to persuade me that life was still worth living. A recent tragic loss had left it empty.

As the Cyril of his own story, Lawrence played a thin part, but other characters stood out vividly. Most haunting to me was *Emily*, daughter of Strelley Mill Farm. There were personal descriptions of her:

Her head was bare, and her black hair, soft and short and ecstatic, tumbled wildly into loose, light curls. She thrust the stalks of the berries under her combs. Her hair was not heavy or long enough to have held them. Then, with the ruby bunches glowing through the black mist of curls, she looked at me brightly, with wide eyes.[1]

And again:

Some people, instead of bringing with them clouds of glory, trail clouds of sorrow; they are born with the gift of sorrow. Sorrows, they proclaim, alone are real. Sorrow is beauty, and the supreme blessedness. You read it in their eyes, and in the tones of their voices. Emily had the gift of sorrow. It fascinated me, but it drove me to rebellion.[2]

Lawrence told me that "Emily" was a portrait of the girl friend of his boyhood and youth. A little later he brought me a short story[3] he had just written. It began with the sentence "Muriel has sent me some mauve primroses" and contained quotations from "Muriel's" letter accompanying them. I began to realise something of the part that Jessie Chambers played in his life.

In July 1910 she came to spend a week-end in Croydon, where Lawrence was a master in Davidson Road elementary school. (Then and subsequently, "Muriel" was the name for her tacitly accepted by us all; she used it as signature on her letters.) The three of us went to Hayes Common for a walk on the Sunday afternoon. I found her as vivid as the picture Lawrence had drawn of her, but she had a warmth and strength of personality he had not suggested. Her short, soft, dark curls flouted the convention

[1] D. H. Lawrence, *The White Peacock* (Wm. Heinemann, London, 1911).

[2] *Ibid.*

[3] Subsequently published under the title of "The Fly in the Ointment" in *Early Life of D. H. Lawrence* by Ada Lawrence and G. Stuart Gelder (London, Martin Secker, 1932), p. 183.

of a hat and belied the firm lines of her nose and chin. She was tanned as a gipsy, and wore a claret-red frock of simple cut that suited her colouring. She greeted me with perception and sympathy. Lawrence had talked as frankly to her of me as to me of her; and she knew that he was concentrating upon the tragedy in which I had been involved, and making it the theme of his second work.

She was then twenty-four, Lawrence twenty-five, and I twenty-eight. We had passions in common—reverence for the Word as literature, and the reality it expressed, hatred for the superficiality and falseness of the age in which we lived, delight in the search for clear definition and the illuminating phrase. Between Jessie Chambers and myself there developed a unique bond based upon our mutual recognition of Lawrence's genius. I came to understand how she had fostered that genius, unconsciously, by the intensity of her own spirit. She had made the demand it initially required, and provided the plane upon which it could function—services no one else within the circle of his early environment could have rendered.

On this Sunday afternoon of our first meeting we returned to Lawrence's Addiscombe lodging for tea. In the absence of his hostess, Jessie prepared the meal, with the grace of humility which distinguished her. Lawrence's happy mood of the early afternoon had changed; he sprawled on the hearthrug castigating a book of modern verse. Jessie was gentle—she treated him rather as Mary of Bethany might have treated Christ. He reacted irritably; the harmony of the day was gone, and I left as soon as tea was over. Late that evening, having seen Jessie to the railway station, Lawrence called at my home, and finding me alone, went straight to the subject of his relationship with her. They were, he said, tacitly engaged, but his mother was inimical to Jessie and would never, he knew, give her consent to the marriage. Nor was he always certain, in spite of their great and significant friendship, that he wanted Jessie as his wife.

During the August holidays Lawrence wrote to me from his home—a letter in great sprawling characters, utterly unlike his usual neat hand-writing. It was full of torment, of pity for Jessie, with whom he felt he must definitely break, and of contempt for his own indecision.

Muriel met me. She is very pretty and very wistful . . . I have promised to go there to-morrow, to stay till Thursday. If I have the courage I shall not stay . . . I must tell her that we ought finally and definitely to part—if I have the heart to tell her.

That letter showed me a new David Lawrence, who came to me not as Life's ambassador, but as a soul torn between conflicting loyalties, each so exacting that he would have me venture to weight the balance on one or the other side. Before I had fully grasped this situation, the development of the mother's fatal illness pulled the balance down, finally. The least thing—the only thing the son felt he could do in the presence of her suffering—was to defer to her judgment, to endorse her standard of values, to deny Jessie Chambers. He began to write the story of Paul Morel; it was to be his mother's justification and apotheosis; and he made a proposal of marriage to a girl of his mother's world.

Since our meeting in July, Jessie and I had exchanged letters. Her letters confirmed my original impression of her rare quality and intuitional power. They also reflected the suffering inflicted upon her by the long conflict with Lawrence. Their conflict was inevitable; social principle and the inheritance of a sternly Puritan moral code obliged her to dismiss, as intolerable, the suggestion of a physical intimacy less binding than that of marriage; nor did she lack the desire of the normal woman for a unique personal right in the man to whom she would devote her life.

In early October she wrote:

> I have just read David's poems in the Review.[4] That first one is the very accent of the David I knew until a few months ago. Times and times without number he has left me to walk over a wet meadow with water on one hand and black woods on the other, and all heaven and earth shaken in my soul. And every time before I reached home I had fought and wrestled with the intangible, and found a heaven in my heart, a fighting heaven—a regular Valhalla except for the feasting.
>
> He talks to me so distinctly from that printed page that it is only with difficulty I can restrain myself from answering him; the effort to restrain gives me a rending sensation. But we have talked like that long enough—let it go. Nevertheless it seems strange. I find myself wondering stupidly what has happened. I look at his portrait—the one he likes so much—I seek in his features for a clue to the puzzle, but shake my head; the portrait lacks the swift changes of expression.
>
> David is my Sodom and Gomorrah. Like Abram, I seek in vain for the five just men. Nay, I am reduced to looking for *one* just man. I do find one just man, of noble stature; he is essential truth, like the truth in the poems. But the lovable men of everyday, common, human truth and honour, they are not to be found, and that one great noble man is not able to save the cities; rather he is likely to be lost in their ruins . . . I always suspected that those dear human souls had no home in my cities, but I could not enquire very closely, because I was overshadowed by the noble austerity of one exceedingly just man. But now it is difficult; the cities crave for the strength of their smaller members; they have become democratic.
>
> You will forgive me that I am so troublesome. You are another star in my bowl, one that neither David nor I saw when he wrote that poem.

---

[4] *The English Review,* edited by Ford Madox Hueffer, to whom she had submitted, a year earlier, the first of Lawrence's poems to appear in print. The poems referred to above were "End of Another Home Holiday" and "In the Boat."

The Chambers family had left the Haggs Farm, described by Lawrence in *The White Peacock*. Mr. Chambers was now farming land that lay between Mapperley Plains, north-west of Nottingham, and the mining village of Arnold. The farm, known as Arno Vale, was an agricultural outpost, doomed, in less than thirty years, to be overcome by the industrial expansion of the city. Nottingham and Arnold are now linked by streets of suburban houses crossing the Vale. In 1910 the old farmhouse, hidden in a green hollow, was approached from the Plains by a steep and irregular footpath winding through hilly pasture. The path ended by the gate of the orchard fronting the house. Stackyard, cowsheds, stable, and barns lay behind.

Two of Jessie Chambers' brothers farmed with their father, a younger sister worked in the house with her mother. Jessie was an assistant mistress in one of the Nottingham Educational Authority's new schools, situated in the southern suburb of West Bridgford. Her superior education, work, and literary trend tended to isolate her from the everyday life of her family. The old farm-house, picturesque but inconvenient, demanded the unending toil of her mother and sister; but the mother, with a gentle, ironic pride, discouraged Jessie from participation in rough and dirty work.

If Jessie had, as Lawrence said, "the gift of sorrow," Mrs. Chambers had the gift of submission. She, physically unsuited to a life of hard domestic labour, hugged the austerity of her lot, and would not be spared. The uneven brick floor of the big farm kitchen must be scrubbed over daily. The white tiles of the hearth below the open range must be cleared and re-washed morning and afternoon, though the ashes fell again on them immediately. In general, Jessie Chambers loved her home, but hated it for the immolation of her mother. When the men of the family tramped into the newly-washed kitchen, the mud of the stackyard thick on the heavy boots they were never asked to leave outside, her colour would heighten with suppressed anger: yet always she checked the protest that rose to her lips, knowing that the sensitive little mother could not endure it.

She would have me spend a week-end at Arno Vale in October, and a week of the Christmas holidays. Between these two visits of mine had come the break in her close association with Lawrence, consequent upon his engagement.

On December 18th she wrote:

This morning I went to High Pavement Unitarian Chapel. It is the only place of worship in Nottingham where I feel, in any sense, at home. It stands in the midst of the lace-market, only a few yards from the house where my grand-mother—mother's mother—was brought up. The preacher was Lloyd Thomas, a very well-known man . . . His text was "Be ye therefore perfect, even as your Father which is in Heaven is perfect." He said, very quietly but with deep emphasis, "We've got to attain this perfection. It's the last word on sociology and on economics, and it's got to be attained, either on this planet or on some other." I could hardly help smiling at his deep, quiet conviction.

When you come you shall see some new writing of mine, if we can remember it and have any time. It is an attempt that I shall truly try to carry to a termination. I have got into the seventh folio, which is a critical stage with me.

Do you remember the hour of your arrival here on the Sunday we came down together? It is just about that time now, and the sky is pale gold through the big window, and blue-grey mist through the little one that looks over the crew-yard. The sunshine to-day has seemed so precious I could almost long to go out and gather an armful of gold before it all sinks behind the high hedge. But I am not so impetuous nowadays; I know that the sun is faithful.

I did hear from David. I saw him also, last Sunday. I suppose you will have seen him by now. I think I must not talk about him at all. At present I am not strong enough. If an artery were cut, you would tie up the end of it, wouldn't you! Well, I must not undo the band, lest I could never get it on again.

It is wonderful how strangely old sayings come back with stores of new meaning. The sins of the parents visited upon the children—well, it is so—and who can help it! Because my forebears had a terrible degree of intensity, nobody can help that it should be handed on to me. And David is strangled in his mother's tragedy; he has to pay the cost for her. So we have to pay our dues, and it isn't much use talking . . . But many things become extraordinarily full of meaning which used to be very dim.

Sunny days with night snow-showers and hard frost framed the after-Christmas holidays at Arno Vale. My most vivid memories are those of the evenings. There was early supper with the whole family in the big kitchen, with spasmodic talk and awkward silences—the young Midlanders were shy of the foreign, southern guest. When it was over, Jessie Chambers took me across the hall into the farm-house parlour, now tacitly recognised as her study. The rich glow of a fire piled high in the old-fashioned grate gleamed on the mossy trunks of fruit trees visible through the square-paned windows. When the table lamp was lit, a portrait of Lawrence, and one of his drawings, appeared on the parlour wall. Jessie Chambers became indubitably "Muriel." She would wheel forward the red settee, and since I could not be persuaded to lie on it, would bring also to the fireside the Duchess's low chair (which had a romantic story, and discovered to the family, soon after purchase, the Duchess's embroidery scissors at the back of its seat).

Jessie and I were so much attuned that we could talk frankly of intimate matters, read one another's written work, or just remain silent, listening to the rustle of a light snow on the panes and the flicker of the fire. Now I read the first section of my friend's novel, arrived, as she had said, at its seventh chapter. This section presented the study of a sensitive childhood—the moving study of a young soul too early awake to the beauty and terror of existence. She had called it, provisionally, "The Rathe

Primrose." I begged her to continue it. Other short stories, based upon family history and her own experience, she showed me, but no poetry and no imaginative work. She wrote with simplicity and a delicate realism, drawing her material chiefly from home life.

Our holiday ended with three days' walking in Derbyshire. The first night we spent at the cottage of Jessie's married sister May. The last night of that strange, transitional year 1910 saw us tramping the dark road to Matlock Bank, the Trent tearing alongside over its unseen, rocky bed. Then an unbelievable funicular railway swung us up to the door of a dimly-lit, nearly deserted hydro, and we looked down from the high window of a big, ice-cold room at starry clustering lights in a valley as deeply inscrutable as the dark sky.

In February Jessie wrote:

I have been wishing you were here all to-day and yesterday. Arno is looking more charming than I think you have ever seen it. A sprinkling of snow lifts the outlines of the hills into prominence, and under the sunshine our valley is brilliant and glittering. The ponds are frozen; I have been sliding on them; the lower pond, with the branches of a willow drooping over the ice, brings back to me the far end of the mill-pond at Felley Mill, as David and I found it one winter day.

I dread Spring, yet look forward to it. I am happy in the repose of Winter, when all is sealed and sleeping, and the wonder of nature is only superficial. Yet I look for snowdrops piercing the soil, and the thought of daffodil bulbs lying buried gives me a sudden breathless feeling, and I watch for Spring with love and dread.

Oh, I wish we could establish some means of communication other than this of sitting down to frame words! Why can't I, watching the log blaze, and having so many things to say to you, just capture your thought. It seems so natural and so simple. I used to think I could really effect it with David; I believe, at times, we did manage it. The snapping of that cord with David was the strangest of all things in

the break with him, and has made more difference to me than anything
else—it has given me psychic freedom.

How curious these things are!

During 1911 Lawrence and Jessie Chambers seldom met, but
he wrote often to her, and begged her to write to him. She needed
no urging, for she now saw him as the rudderless ship of her
own imagery. His mother's death, while leaving him without direction, had not freed him from maternal compulsions. He had
died with his mother, but Jessie's mood reflected her faith that he
might in time come to new birth, and liberty of spirit . . . Lawrence's own mood was one of frustration, which the reception ac-
corded his novel did little to dispel. "I *did* think it would have
given me a start," he said to me disconsolately, as we picked April
primroses in Farleigh Woods. It had, but there was no immediate public recognition of a new genius. Moreover, he was now
realising that marriage with a girl of his mother's world would
never link him safely and permanently into that world; and that
his engagement had been a mistake. It dragged on, however, until
the beginning of 1912, when apparently his fiancée came to the
same conclusion.

Jessie had no challenge to offer in the matter of my friendship
with Lawrence; between us there was a rare and complete confi-
dence. She was glad that my home, where she was welcomed by
my parents during school holidays, was also open to him on the
school-day evenings. Lawrence spent his holidays in Eastwood or
elsewhere, so they did not cross one another's path in Croydon.
Once during this year she wrote to me:

> What an extraordinary situation, unattempted as yet in fiction: you
> come to me directly from David; you step from me into the presence-
> chamber of David. I wonder how it affects you, the swift transition
> from one individuality to another.

The south of England was terrain as fresh to Jessie as the Midlands to me, so when she came to visit me I must needs take her into Sussex, lead her over the South Downs, and show her, from a wind-sheltered hollow on Seaford Head, the foam-fringed beaches and the little old sea-port of my childhood's happiest days. Or we would spend days in London, visiting art galleries, listening to great music at Queen's Hall, riding on the upper, un-roofed decks of 'buses, watching and sensing the infinite variety of life that seethed through the city. Jessie's approach to art was one of delight and reverence, and music was an illumination that enhanced the dark beauty of her eyes; but she looked on London almost fearfully.

I remember [she wrote in August, 1914], on that same evening, the glitter of London, the brilliance that I have never been able to see without a tremor. It seems to me so unstable; so gigantic and so frail. I think perhaps I have always felt like that, because, long before I saw London I was impregnated with the idea of its colossal injustice, the enormity of the contrast between its two opposite poles.

We always carried a book on these occasions, to be read to-gether in the train or tram, on a seat in the park, or when waiting for a meal. In this way we read, this year, among other books, the ten volumes of Romain Rolland's recently published *Jean Chris-tophe,* borrowed from the Croydon public library, Maeterlinck's *Treasure of the Humble,* and Chesterton's *Orthodoxy.* But every-thing read seemed to bear some fantastic relation to the enigma of Lawrence.

The Whitsun holidays saw me again at Arno Vale. I travelled by the night excursion train, and have a vivid memory of arrival at 5 A.M. in the bright sunshine of a May morning. Jessie met me at Nottingham station, and the first tram of the day swung us up to Mapperley Plains. From the old stile on the Breck Hill lane we looked down on Arno in its hollow, a faint mist still entangled in its blossoming apple orchard; and we descended the narrow path

through pastures set for hay and starred with marguerites . . .
Summer came, and August brought the long holidays from
school, and the beginning of corn harvest . . . One afternoon we
sat reading on a pile of dry straw in the stackyard. Someone
called, "Mind! the bull's loose!" but the operation known as
"pulling one's leg" was not unknown on the farm, and we ignored the warning. Suddenly I found myself looking straight into
the eyes of the bull, which had approached unseen, hidden by the
wall of the stack. I, like a city-bred fool, jumped up and ran off,
frightening the creature, which turned and faced about; Jessie
rose slowly and followed it out of the stackyard; it went quietly,
and was shut in its stall.

During these months Lawrence was re-writing the opening section of "Paul Morel" (ultimately published as *Sons and Lovers*).
Jessie completed about two-thirds of "The Rathe Primrose," but
discarded this title in favour of *Eunice Temple*. (The initials of
the second title she used as a pseudonym when publishing her
book *D. H. Lawrence; A Personal Record,* in 1935.)

The letter following is dated September 11th, 1911:

Your letter gives me to feel so poignantly the breadths of the
Downs and the silence of the larchwood that I am moved to reply on
the instant. I was about to write to you myself of the moon-mist of
that self-same evening—Wednesday, to wit—but that I seized the opportunity of talking business matters with father for the relief of my
own mind.

I don't think he feels acutely the loss of his mother; she had lived
her life and longed to die. He will, as time passes, become aware of a
blank that as yet he hardly suspects. No! he is moved by the mingled
romance and sordidness of the money matters of the family. He has no
eye for realism; he moves with the drama and is attracted by a certain
glamour that clothes almost all human dealing for him. It is our one
strong point of contact—we warm over it instantly. He changes as we
talk; he takes on a refinement of perception, and he employs a new

vocabulary. Such a *rapprochement* will sustain a thread of sympathy between us for weeks. But I, ungrateful realist that I am, refuse to support the illusion. What fate makes me ask for consistency?

This is a month of marvellous mornings, and evenings that would once have made me ache for their beauty. They *are*, now. Fact, reality, part of my life, like my thoughts, like poetry, things mine for always. It is a curious change, to be able to laugh at the loveliness of evenings and mornings; to be sure of them and proud in them.

I wish you could see our orchard. Red apples, strung like coral along the boughs, intense against the blue sky. Firm to one's teeth and sweet. I should like you to have some. I have asked David if he can suggest a good way of sending some to you jointly—not through the post . . . This week the wall of corn is to be attacked—we are threshing for several days.

David has his cake by now I expect. If you happen to share it, give me your critical opinion.

(The cake, of her own making, was a birthday gift to Lawrence.)

At the beginning of this winter of 1911 Lawrence developed pneumonia. The illness ended his teaching career. He had now some prospect of literary success; *The Trespasser*, his second novel, had been accepted by Messrs. Duckworth, and Martin Secker had asked for a book of short stories. After convalescence in Bournemouth he returned to Eastwood, intending to finish *Sons and Lovers* there.

Jessie wrote to me in early February, just before his return. (She was then working steadily at her own book, having received encouragement from Edward Garnett, to whom I had submitted for criticism one of her short stories. Edward Garnett had a reputation for sound criticism, and was known to have sponsored the early work of both John Galsworthy and Joseph Conrad. "I find Miss Chambers' work full of fine quality and true feeling," Garnett had written to me—and he enclosed with his letter a recommendation to be forwarded to Austin Harrison, then editor of *The English Review*.) Her letter ran:

It is just after tea; the house is very quiet, the juicy wood on my fire keeps up a little hissing song. The sky over the poplars is very bright, with bars of vivid cloud, and over the orchards are soft masses of fantastic shape, dragons and radiant angels.

I am writing *The Rathe Primrose* afresh, and as I get back into the small circle of intense emotion and passionate beliefs I feel, by contrast, a lonely aimless creature. How badly we need a religion in this life of ours! And what a fate to have been born in such an age of transition! To have nothing to worship is old age, and all the world is like that now. I wonder, shall we succeed in evolving a new religion! For it is the supreme task of this and of the ages to follow. The cry for a new religion sounds the deepest note in all the Labour struggles, for why does the democracy crave greater freedom from the animal burden of existence except from the inborn and immortal desire to find expression for its spiritual part in life!

I wish that I had one pursuit as absorbing as you have in your music; it is very good to have a dominant note. But the only satisfying thing in life is an impersonal aim, which pre-supposes an ideal; which again rests upon religion.

I wonder if you will like this little Verlaine. If you don't like him, don't have him . . . I send also two views of Arno; you will like them.

Lawrence's early draft of *Sons and Lovers* was less autobiographical and more fictional than the published novel. Jessie Chambers tells how he sent her the unfinished manuscript during the autumn of 1911, asking for her comments. She thought the opening section lacking in spontaneity, and the factual and fictional threads ill woven. She suggested that he should delete the inventions, and tell the story of his mother and his home life and adolescence as simple fact. She admits that in the back of her mind was the thought that Lawrence, by this exercise, might free himself from his mother-complex. He agreed with her suggestion.

After the interlude of his illness, and the termination of his life in Croydon, Lawrence returned to Eastwood with a mind at leisure to re-create the past, and a will to absorb again the home atmosphere. His mother, though dead, was still dominant, still enshrined here in the heart of her family; it carried on in her tradition, it used her phrase. Every crock on the dresser, every piece of furniture, had known her touch . . . She seemed as near, while he sat writing of her, as if she were only out for a morning's shopping. He threw himself with avidity into the realisation of her strong, combative personality, and felt again the compelling force of her direction. He wrote rapidly, with conviction.

When Jessie Chambers received the first instalments of his new draft she was impressed with its vividness and power. The scenes from his childhood and adolescence were faithfully, graphically described. But the working out of the relationship between "Paul" and "Miriam" was a terrible distortion of the truth as she conceived it. The "Miriam" of the new writing, bearing her likeness, placed in her known environment, was not she, but her image as reflected in the distorting mirror of Mrs. Lawrence's mind. This image the publication of *Sons and Lovers* would broadcast, not only to an external reading public, but to her own family, friends, and acquaintances. Its perpetuation was the son's final gesture of surrender to the maternal will. There remained one other compulsion upon him—the sacrifice must be sealed by the pre-knowledge and acceptance of "Miriam" herself. He must convince her of its justice.

Lawrence's last approaches to Jessie Chambers were vain attempts to gain her acquiescence and submission. For the first time her reaction was repulsion. By this betrayal of her faith in him he had defaced his own image—the image she had carried throughout the years of their friendship—that "one just man of noble stature" who was "essential truth." She saw him now as a slave, subordinate once and for all to his mother's will and influence. She could not bear the sight, and turned away from him.

It was at this crucial moment of his life that Lawrence met a woman fully equipped by temperament and circumstance to re-lease him from the maternal bondage. Frieda was the sun of a new day, whose beams dispelled the dark atmospheres of his youth. She came with strength, like a being from a superior world, and called him to her; her superb faith in his genius re-stored his self-confidence. Soon he was in Europe with Frieda, walking in her light and warmth, the compulsions of the old home sunken below his horizon.

But Jessie Chambers had to work out, alone, a reorientation of her spirit; there was no change of personnel, scene, or circum-stances to help the process. She felt that a cataclysm had torn away a vital section of her world. The shrunken sphere must be rounded, and if it were not to disintegrate, it must be kept mov-ing in conformity with the other spheres of its universe. The effort at readjustment called for all her vitality.

Our correspondence continued, but the spontaneity and lyric-ism disappeared from her letters. Of Lawrence she told me only that he had finished his novel and had gone to Germany; a year passed before the whole position was made clear to me. During the summer of 1912 I saw, with a strange and hurting sense of loss, a change in her which amounted indeed to a modification of the personality I had known as "Muriel." The lamp of her spirit burned low; vision and desire failed. She turned with loathing from her own writing, and with one exception, mentioned below, read no books. Her fine poise, her quiet self-confidence left her; she moved as if in an enemy world, warily. The savour of her conversation was irony. The consciousness of an intimate under-standing between us blurred; she became defensive. It seemed that her soul had withdrawn to its innermost fortification—the drawbridge was up, the portcullis down.

We had planned an August holiday in the Rhineland. It was an empty experience. With all the beauty of the mid-reaches of the Rhine in sunshine about her, Jessie sat absorbed in Dostoievsky's classic study of human decadence and decay *The Brothers Karamazov*. We walked together in the illuminated grounds of the Kurhaus in Wiesbaden, among the vast buildings of ancient Mainz, and by the banks of the Neckar, but all the time I felt, curiously, that I was alone.

In later years I came to understand. Jessie Chambers had seen me, originally (as I had first seen her) pictured by the mind of Lawrence. His agency had brought about our meeting, and though a personal friendship had grown between us, its inspiration was still Lawrence. During 1911, when he and she seldom met, I had served as a link between them. It was inevitable that she, reacting against him, should also turn from me. Only in severance from Lawrence and his whole environment did she feel that she could escape identification with the image he had written into *Sons and Lovers*.

In the Spring of the following year Lawrence sent her proofs of the novel. She returned them to him without comment. To me she wrote:—

A gale is blowing, buffetting my windows. It is hurting; I feel as if I had been buffetted all night— there is the soreness and aching in my limbs as if I had been beaten by the blind inhuman force of the wind.

Yesterday morning came the proofs of *Sons and Lovers*. I can't think why David wished me to read them, since nothing now can be altered. All this turmoil of emotion makes me fearfully sick—I can neither eat nor sleep, and sit in front of the fire shivering as if I had ague. Indeed, after reading that accursed writing I am as flabby as even David could wish to portray me.

The "Miriam" part of the novel is a slander—a fearful treachery. David has interpreted her every word, action and thought in the light of "Mrs. Morel's" hatred of her . . . I believe, with entire conviction, that David's mind is, in a subtle way, unhinged. He has swung to so violent a reaction from his earlier, rather beautiful self that in one direction he has exceeded.

I think the story would be painful, even to a stranger. At the end one feels no further—only shocked and dismayed at the tragedy and brutality of it all.

Don't talk about it, please. If I am to live at all it will be necessary to put David out of my life—to ignore him entirely, in thought and speech. Please, please digest this quickly and get it over before I come.

She came at Easter, only to find that the attempt to find a new basis for our friendship was hopeless. She could not dissociate me from the conception of Lawrence, and after three painful days she returned home. The kaleidoscope of our lives had been shaken, the familiar patterns destroyed, and new patterns were taking shape. A few days after her return she wrote:

I have brought back out of last week a large number of exquisite moments. Sudden aspects of the Shirley road between the trees, of the valley beyond Purley, of that superb slope just outside the little spinney off the main road to Oxted. Then Oxted itself, sunny and sleeping, the crowded sheep-pen, the rare magic of Limpsfield in the silver dusk. These things now seem exalted and linked like beads on a chain of strange, exquisite pain, a peculiar exhaustion that still keeps the faculty of perception. I don't know how it all comes about.

Her August holiday she spent in France, staying a few days in Paris, and then going to a farm in Bordeaux, the home of a former pen-friend, the schoolmaster son of a peasant freeholder. The slow, instinctive, un-selfconscious life of the French farm soothed and strengthened her. She sent me impressions of her new experiences.

I liked wandering about Paris, particularly in the Latin quarter, where every other shop is a bookshop, and the streets have a certain significant quiet. The most entirely lovely place I have seen is without doubt La Sainte Chapelle, which is part of the Palais de Justice. It is quite small, and is kept as one would keep an exquisite jewel-case, simply for its beauty. To step into the blue and gold gloom of the chapel from the sunshine of the courtyard is marvellous. It is all blue and gold, deep, rich colour, making a kind of liquid light, an essence. Then up a short flight of stairs to the Chapelle superieure, where tall Gothic windows, from floor to ceiling, distil a gorgeous mist of colour, purple, green, red, and the richest blue I have ever seen. All the supports are gold, the window jambs and the slender pillars reaching up into a mystery and wonder of colour. There is nothing whatever in the chapel, it is just the exquisite shell. When I come to my last memory of life I should like it to be the memory of the *chapelle superieure* in La Sainte Chapelle.

The people here are simple, rather primitive, and very courteous. There are Marc's father and mother, his grandmother, and his aunt— a widow—one of the most intelligent women I have ever met. She is exceedingly dramatic, and full to the brim of life. From the very first I have been able to talk to her. She has very dark, very keen brown eyes, and she laughs, as indeed everybody does, enormously. Marc's mother goes sometimes to Mass. I asked Tante if she also went. She shook her head. "Vous êtes libre-penseuse?" I asked. Her face became very serious. "Mon pauvre mari était libre-penseur, et je le suis. Je l'ai suivi ici, et je le suivrai là bas."

I am very happy here. The life is different, but not so different from, say, life at the Haggs. The people are close to the bases of life, and are direct and genuine. They are all extremely good to me. They laugh at me, but good-naturedly.

Jessie Chambers returned from France with a quiet spirit and a bias towards the more instinctive and unsophisticated forms of life. In this mood she met the farmer's son who became her companion of the next two years, and whom in 1915 she married.

She and I seldom met after her marriage, and correspondence

between us was infrequent. She devoted herself to her home and her husband's interests. The manuscript of the novel, *Eunice Temple,* was ultimately destroyed.

In March, 1930, the world heard of Lawrence's death. Shortly after, Jessie wrote:

> I see from the papers that D. H. L. has finished his earthly course. It was a great shock to me because I did not know that he was ill. Have you kept in touch with him of late years and can you tell me anything about him? I never resumed any correspondence, so I have no personal knowledge of him whatsoever, but I feel for him as deeply as in the old days, and if you know anything of him you would care to pass on, I shall be glad to hear it. My impression is that he suffered deeply and blindly at the hands of life. Have you seen him at all of late years, and do you know when he was last in England? It is strange to think he no longer sees the sunshine and the great clouds upon the skies of March. Let us hope his angry spirit has found peace, which I think he did not find on earth.

I could tell her little, having had no contact with Lawrence, personal or by letter, since 1913; but a friend recently in touch with him had given me some details of his last months. I sent these. She replied:

> Thank you for your letter, and also for the extract from that of the friend who knew him in his illness. It confirms my own intuitions.
>
> Of late, this last year or so, I have been conscious of a growing desire to write to him . . . but I did not trust my intuition sufficiently to act. Since then—all the autumn, I was aware of a strange drawing near —but there is a sad lack of correspondence between the outer and the inner life, and still I did not send him that message of friendliness and affection that something prompted me to do. Strangely enough, I never thought of him as ill, and likely to die. I had such a feeling that the business between us was not finished.
>
> Some time in 1928 mother heard that he was ill, and persuaded my

brother to write to him. The reply[5] was a little lyric of love and affection to us all. It is dated November 28th, 1928, but I heard of it only a week ago. They did not tell me for fear of upsetting me. You see, people have always believed they knew better what was good for us in our relations to one another than we did ourselves! How right they were, let posterity judge!

I think his message was that we should obey the inner light, but he got it all hopelessly wrong. When I remember how despairingly he used to tell me he *could not* do without me in his artistic life, I feel terribly guilty. But what I did I had to do: there was no choice in the matter. And during all these eighteen years of separation there has been on my part a tremendous effort to understand, to get some sort of a meaning out of all that happened. Something is achieved, that I am certain. If only one realises how inexorable is life, that is something. For him, I cannot speak. The only book of his I have read, MSS apart, is *Twilight in Italy,* which I have quite forgotten, and some short stories, which I thought utterly unworthy of him. Poor D. H. L. —and yet how wonderful he was! It is good to know that such a spirit can take human form; if it falls short of the glory of God, well, that is in God's hands too. He has helped me to extend enormously the territory of life and that is a godlike thing to do.

In 1933 I sent her a copy of my just published essay *Lawrence and* APOCALYPSE. She acknowledged this in the last of her letters to me.

I'm sorry to be rather late in returning the book,[6] but the spring cleaning was fairly long and exhausting, and gave time neither for reading nor writing. Now it is over, and I am rejoicing in a clean house and a little leisure.

Well, your book will rank along with the other Laurentian literature: it is a document; and if it bears witness to the author rather than to the subject of the work it is not the less interesting and significant.

---

[5] See *The Letters of D. H. Lawrence,* ed. Aldous Huxley (London, Wm. Heinemann, 1932), p. 761.

[6] Not *L. & A.*—but a book lent previously to J. C.

I can't wax enthusiastic about it, because it is concerned with that aspect of D. H. L. that I have always found least interesting. As an artist, when he is dealing with the immediate and the concrete, he is superb, but when he assays to be a thinker I find him superficial and unconvincing, and quite soon boring. The *Revelation* of John of Patmos, and *Apocalypse* of D. H. L. can never have anything but a secondary interest for me.

I have never been able to read the biblical Revelation—when I have tried, I have soon felt that here was the basis for all the Old Moore's Almanacs that ever existed and the guesses and speculations and the monstrous beasts are only wearisome. As a fragmentary and mutilated account of mankind's early attempts to understand his place in the universe, it *is interesting, but that was not really D. H. L.'s concern* with *Revelations*. His concern was to find some means of escape from the narrow prison of his own ego, and to do that he was prepared to assault the cosmos. So, whenever I read his almost delirious denunciations of what he pretended to regard as Christianity, I only see the caged panther lashing himself into a fury to find some way out of his strait prison. D. H. L. was a man in bondage, and all his theorisings and philosophisings only bear witness to his agony.

The more I ponder upon his life and his death, the more significant becomes to me the fact of his suffering—of course I don't mean his physical suffering, *that* was the direct outcome of his spiritual anguish at his own frustration. Well, why was he frustrated, and why was he in bondage? Some of his own words come into my mind. The day before his mother's funeral we went a walk together, and during that walk I reproached him for having become engaged to X.

I said, "You ought not to have involved X in the tangle of our relationships." D. H. L.'s reply took my breath away; he said, "With *should* and *ought* I have nothing to do." If you will think out the implications of that statement you will see what was the nature of D. H. L.'s bondage; he was the measure of his own universe; his own god—and also his own hell. He deliberately (or perhaps he couldn't help it)—anyhow he regarded himself as exempt from the laws that hold mankind together (I am not referring to conventional morality) and when a human being does that, he is of necessity cut off from contact with his fellows.

It seemed to me that D. H. L.'s great powers, far from exempting him from responsibility, conferred upon him a much greater and higher order of responsibility. I could only think that time would prove this. At the end of that same walk, as we stood within a stone's throw of the house where his mother lay dead, he said to me:

"You know, J., I've always loved mother."

"I know you have," I replied.

"I don't mean that," he answered. "I've loved her—like a lover—that's why I could never love you."

Then he handed me the three poems he had written since she died. I think this partly explains why he had placed himself beyond ordinary human sanctions. He was, as it were, driven out of the land of the living into a fearful wilderness of egoism. It explains, too, why, as you remark in your book, he looked in woman only for the animal—female—qualities. It made his dilemma a cruel one, because it compelled him to deny what was best in himself. Consequently his prison was also a terrible battleground where his two selves were constantly fighting each other.

I don't propose to write a book about him, and yet I know an aspect of his life that no one else has known or can possibly know. So I hope to leave a simple historical record, so that if at some future time some biographer with no preconceived theories about him but a genuine desire to find out what manner of man he was, and what forces went to his making should arise, my record will exist as one of the "sources." That, I feel, I owe to D. H. L., and to what he stood for. But I loathe exhibitionism, so that only a later generation will read my record, if, indeed, it is ever read.

Strangely enough, the record will extend just beyond his death, and perhaps you will be interested to hear that part. As I have said, the fact of D. H. L.'s suffering is the dominant fact of his life for me, but it was only after the publication of *The Plumed Serpent* that I realised he was a tortured spirit. As you know, I returned his last letter in 1913, and since then no word ever passed between us, and I never heard news of him; his name was never mentioned to me. I did not know that he was ill; the letter he sent to my brother was never shown to me until weeks after his death, so that whatever knowledge I had of him came through other channels than those of ordinary communication. For some eighteen months or so before his death I felt acutely drawn to him at times, and wondered intensely how some kind of communication, that seemed so urgently needed, was to be established. It seemed to be not just a matter of writing a letter. The feeling that some drawing together was imminent scarcely ever left me. Once, quite suddenly, as though he had spoken, the words came into my mind—"We are still on the same planet." There were other things, too, of a like nature. Please remember that I had no idea D. H. L. was ill. On the morning of the day he died, he suddenly said to me, as distinctly as if he had been here in the room with me, "Can you remember only the pain and none of the joy?" And his voice was so full of reproach that I made haste to assure him that I *did* remember the joy. Then later, in a strange, confused way he said—"What has it all been about?"

The next morning I was busy with my housework when suddenly the room was filled with his presence and for a moment I saw him just as I had known him in early days, with the little cap on the back of his head. That momentary presence was so full of joy that I simply concluded it was an earnest of a real meeting in the near future. I remember saying to myself, "Now I *know* we're going to meet."

The following day his death was announced in the papers, and was a terrible shock to me. I give you this for what it is worth . . . smile it away if you will, it doesn't matter; the experience was just as real as the fact that I am now holding a pen. I don't think it was self-suggestion, because I didn't know he was ill; I was full of anxiety on his behalf, but I judged his trouble to be of the soul.

I am sure that he broke through his prison before the end, and died a free spirit, though he had lived in bondage. I think his last poems show that he found the way to freedom and wholeness, so that he achieved a triumph, but not the kind he used to write about so much. It had been my conviction all along that he would find out what the trouble really was, and I had almost dared to believe that having achieved the inner unity, without which he spent himself in vain, he would be strong enough to reshape his life on positive values; but it was not to be. By the time he understood his malady he had spent his vital force. I was expecting too much from one earthly span; the suffering of self-division to its utmost limit was a lifetime's work, maybe. The story of the unification lies in the future.

So you see this is how D. H. L. appears to me, and his long arguments about aristocrats and democrats and the rest are only the dusty miles he covered in his pilgrimage. The only interest they have for me is the internal evidence they bear as to the state of his soul. Apart from that they are utterly unreal. There is no such thing as a division of people in aristocrats and democrats; it is the same with human beings as with the wheat among which the enemy had sown tares, "Let both grow together till harvest." The only definition of democracy that appeals to me is this: "Democracy is that arrangement of society in which every individual has an opportunity of becoming an aristocrat." . . . "By their fruits shall ye know them."

Again, is that Golden Age of which D. H. L. dreamed in some remote past any further back than his own boyhood and youth? It is a great error to suppose that his early life was unhappy. In our home his name was a synonym for joy—radiant joy in simply being alive. He communicated that joy to all of us, and made us even happy with one another when he was there; no small achievement in a family like ours! No! D. H. L.'s Golden Age was the time up to nineteen or so, before that fatal self-division began to manifest itself. What was it that Keats said about a great man's life being an allegory, and his works a comment on it? Something of that applies to D. H. L. You see that in essentials my feeling has not changed in spite of other deep affection. What he has said about the indestructibility of love is quite true, on a particular plane.

I hope this long letter will not bore you. I haven't said much about your book, but I think you will understand my attitude.

You may like to read Carter's book. I prize it for the little, clean, biographical touches . . . D. H. L. sitting on his heels feeding the fire with sticks—how clearly I see him, and his sombre face. Keep it as long as you like, but some time I'd like to see it again. My very best wishes for the success of your book.

The signature, "Jessie Wood," used for the first time in a letter to me, was a further indication of the distance which had steadily widened between our respective conceptions of Lawrence and his work. I could not accept Jessie's positive diagnosis of schizophrenia, and be satisfied to account in that way for the trend of his development; nor did he seem to me to have lived like "a man in bondage" or "a caged panther." He was indeed profoundly egoistic, and looked within his own soul for his sanctions instead of accepting those of his day and society; so have all great artists. His conflict was the inevitable outcome of his challenging position. But Jessie's possessive love for Lawrence's adolescent self prevented her from appreciating him as an adult— she yearned for the student boy "with the little cap on the back of his head" who had shared what had been her own "Golden Age." The Lawrence of later years she rejected, and repudiated the influences which had modified his life and thought. Though utterly unconscious of the fact, she was repeating the error of Lawrence's mother, who with similar insistence had claimed the boy as she herself was now demanding the youth. Truly, as he had said:
> "ever at my side
>   the beggar-woman, the yearning-eyed
>   inexorable Love goes lagging."

In 1935 the record[7] to which Jessie Wood had referred was published.

---

[7] E. T., *D. H. Lawrence: A Personal Record* (London, Jonathan Cape, 1935).

We met for the last time in 1940. During the March of that year I was staying near Nottingham, and on impulse wrote and suggested a meeting. I had not seen her for seven years. She replied, naming as rendezvous a café in the city. When a bent, heavy figure slowly approached me I recognised her with difficulty and shock. She was recovering, she told me, from a nervous breakdown, which had left her deaf. Shouting over the noise of the crowded café, I tried to get into contact with her, for the dark, intense eyes were still those of "Muriel." It was impossible; as she talked, with smouldering resentment, of the war, of her illness, of the shabby treatment of her book, which had been printed in an American edition without her sanction, I felt emptied of any emotion but pity. Her intuition sensed this at once, and her resentment against an unjust and commercialised literary world flamed against me. Nothing could bridge the gulf between us, and she rose to go, averting her face. We parted, knowing that all was said.

Four years later, and fourteen years after Lawrence's death, that passionate spirit laid down the burden of a suffering and prematurely outworn body. Did it realise again, at the point of its departure, the vision of joy it so greatly desired—the bright-faced, god-like youth, Hermes of the winged sandals, messenger of the Immortals? Who knows? Death is not always as inexorable as life.

CONCERNING

THE WHITE PEACOCK

(from *The Texas Quarterly,* II,
No. 4 [Winter, 1959], 186–190)

THE "NETHERMERE" MS[1] had lain, forgotten, on the shelf of a lumber cupboard in my old home. My father's death shook that home asunder; all the dusty household gods crept blinking from their familiar corners to meet varying fates at the hands of the indifferent. Together with old notebooks, the "Nethermere" MS came back to me.

A pile of blue-lined school paper, covered with D. H. Lawrence's regular script. Parts of chapters transcribed for him by other, recognisable hands—those of friends sympathetic enough to be allowed into the nursery of his first novel. A wavering line runs through its original title, as if he permitted unwillingly the substitution of the name by which the book was published.

I recall my first sight of this manuscript. In February of 1910, D. H. L. is kept in bed by influenza, and I, calling at his lodgings on a raw Saturday afternoon, am sent up to his room. Here is no prophet, no dogmatist, but that wistful spirit, *Cyril*, who slips unobtrusively into the intimate lives of his neighbours. Presently he asks me to give him a brown paper parcel which stands on the

[1] Now in the collection of Mr. George Lazarus. The "sympathetic" friends who copied a portion of the novel from the author's rough draft were Agnes Holt, Agnes Mason, and Jessie Chambers.

floor by the wainscot, apologising, when I lift it, for its weight.
The manuscript has been accepted for publication, he tells me,
but some final revision is necessary. Will I look through it with
an eye for split infinitives and obscurities of phrase? No, I am not
to carry it home myself; he will bring it round tomorrow afternoon. And when I protest he declares that he is quite well again,
and positively refuses to spend another day in bed.

I read the manuscript, with an indifferent mind as to its char-
acterisation, but with an appreciation of its rhythm and rich
colour. At the time, my mental vision was slowly recovering from
the effect of a shock which had stunned, and the people of my
world were scarcely more to me than "trees walking." So the
Lettie of the book, brilliant and wayward, challenged George
Saxton unheeded, the significance of Annesley's story passed me
by, and the other folk might talk and act, but I could not see their
faces. Only *Cyril* I would often follow, as when, on the evening
of Annesley's funeral, he went down to Strelley Mill, "which lay
red and peaceful, with the blue smoke rising as winsomely and
carelessly as ever. On the other side of the valley I could see a pair
of horses nod slowly across the fallow."

How well I knew the sense of detachment that, *in vacuo,* and
from an enormous distance, recorded such things:

The spring came bravely in south London, and the town was filled
with magic.I never knew the sumptuous purples of evening till I saw
the round arc-lamps fill with light and roll like golden bubbles along
the purple dusk of the high road. Everywhere at night the city is filled
with the magic of lamps; over the river they pour in golden patches
their floating luminous oil on the restless darkness; the bright lamps
float in and out of the cavern of London Bridge Station like round,
shining bees in and out of a black hive; in the suburbs the street lamps
glimmer with the brightness of lemons among the trees.

Still more readily could I follow *Cyril* when he returns to the
home valley, after years of absence:

I wandered around Nethermere, which had now forgotten me. The daffodils under the boat-house continued their golden laughter, and nodded to one another in gossip as I watched them, never pausing to notice me . . . I felt like a child left out of the group of my playmates . . . I wanted to be recognised by something . . . I was a stranger, an intruder.

But "Nethermere" was forgotten before the spring of that year broadened into summer. New work was fashioning on the loom of Lawrence's mind, and the weaving went on at great speed—a design patterned in black upon a ground of azure and gold.

When autumn evenings came we sat in my room correcting the proof sheets of *The White Peacock*. But he who flung the sheets impatiently on the floor and cursed the fate that had made him a writer was *Paul Morel*, not *Cyril—Paul*, whose mother was sick unto death. Night and day I carried in my mind the reflection of his heavy, sullen, white face, its steel-dark eyes, set with pain, glinting between narrowed lids.

Some self, realised, dies out of the artist with the completion of every work. *Cyril* died, and *Paul* was born. Was it for *Cyril* that Lawrence inscribed my copy of *The White Peacock* "in memoriam"?

Since then we have gone our separate ways for twenty years, and Lawrence has preceded me into the Silence.[2] And now I take that book and dust away its memories. I will look, with consciousness and intention, at the world of "Nethermere."

The Nottinghamshire valley encloses two mill-ponds, higher and lower, and a lake, broadening between woodlands. At the southern end, Highclose, the house of a local colliery owner, looks across the lake at smaller Woodside, Cyril's home. The

[2] Written in 1930.

farm lands of Strelley Mill lie upon the northern slopes of the valley, which shelters also the incidental manor of a vague squire, a ruined chapel, a keeper's cottage, a disused quarry where, in their season, snowdrops hide. Beyond, to the west, is the mining village, Selsby.

The people of the story live within this little world. True, Lawrence exiles them eventually to Nottingham, to London, to Canada. But the essential drama takes place in the home valley. Here Lettie, "the white peacock," preens herself without a rival to challenge attention; fond mother, devoted brother, and her two lovers, Leslie the gentleman and George the farmer's son, follow her movements and vivid colouring with fascination. She dominates every conversation, is central figure of every social gathering at her home, at Highclose, and at the farm, Strelley Mill. Beside her, in foil, is Emily, the farmer's daughter, dark, sentient, self-mistrustful, the "gift of sorrow" in her eyes, conscious of work-roughened hands, conscious too that her mind has missed the manicuring of the college course which has so obviously polished Lettie's superficial self. A third woman is Meg, the inn-keeper's niece, pretty, simple, unsophisticated, ruthlessly instinctive.

These three women are fully drawn, but Lawrence is not interested in them as individuals. He sees them only in relation to their men. "Take," he would seem to say to his reader, "a male creature! We shall now study its reactions to these various forms of feminine stimuli."

Of the men, George Saxton alone is fully realised. Leslie Tempest is only visible when Lettie illuminates him. Annable the keeper is not so much a man as an incarnate indignation. But one sees the whole George.

There is the curious, insensitive youth who loosens the undeveloped wings of young bees because he wants to know whether the insects will be able to fly. There is the deliberate, imperturbable George who drowns the wounded cat. (I decline to apply the term *callous* to him, since he is obviously reacting against Emily's supersensitiveness.)

There is the bewildered lad who is teased into a temporary consciousness of spiritual values by an excited Lettie whose creative impulses have just awakened.

There is the man who has realised that only Lettie can bring his life to its full fruiting—that she represents for him an essential need; and that he has, through diffidence, lost her. The man who accepts a poor second best in marriage with Meg. . . . And finally there is the George who, unfulfilled, goes rotten. The undeveloped, rotting self of him hangs, mortifying to the living self, contaminating it, spreading death through it.

The stages of degeneration are indicated. George diagnoses his own condition with an explicitness that belongs to his creator. "I wanted something I haven't got. I'm something short. I'm like corn in a wet harvest—full—but pappy—no good. I'll rot. I came too soon; or I wanted something that would have made me grow fierce. That's why I wanted Lettie—I think."

Meg, the instinctive, the unconscious, having secured her motherhood, turns from husband to children. George has become purposeless and a drunkard; she despises him. . . . The final chapters of *The White Peacock* show his last stage, mad drunkenness and subsequent collapse of mind and body. He is sent to stay with his sister Emily, on the lonely farm where she is living a full and happy life with her farmer husband. There Cyril visits him:

Like a tree that is falling, going soft and pale and rotten, clammy with small fungi, he stood leaning against the gate, while the dim afternoon drifted with a flow of thick sweet sunshine past him, not touching him.

They watched the men of the farm stacking wheat:

Then Arthur began to lift the sheaves to the stack, and the two men worked in an exquisite, subtle rhythm . . . Tom, lifted high above the small wagon load, called to his brother some question about the stack. The sound of his voice was strong and mellow. . . . We . . . saw him standing high up on the tallest corner of the stack, as on the prow of a ship.

George watched, and his face slowly gathered expression. He turned to me, his dark eyes alive with horror and despair . . .

"I couldn't team ten sheaves," he said.

"You will in a month or two," I urged.

He continued to watch, while Tom got on the ladder and came down the front of the stack.

"Nay, the sooner I clear out, the better," he repeated to himself.

(But in the "Nethermere" MS George's last words were, originally, *"I've lost it all, I've lost it all!"*)

Jessie Chambers, in her memoir of Lawrence, makes it clear that his first writing of the "Nethermere" story contained no hint of this tragedy of the degenerate. It was a development of the second writing, done during his early days in Croydon. But it was not, I think, a planned development. Lawrence, at the age of twenty-four, was already looking into that dark pool of the subconscious mind from which so many of his later conceptions were drawn. There he saw the image of a potential George, and drew from that image the dominating conclusion of *The White Peacock*. Unless we are to assume that George Saxton was foredoomed by some inherent weakness, Lawrence is using him to establish a general principle. . . .

But what of Lettie, who also accepted the second best, and became an absorbed and contented mother, an efficient wife and hostess?

Behind the woman, safeguarding the woman, stands Erda, the force whose single concern is the perpetuation of the race. In the strength of Erda, and at her prompting, the woman can cut away the dying, unfertilised psyche, so that the reproductive physical self is uncontaminated. But this partial physical self cannot develop individually, and the woman, in motherhood, is absorbed into the lives of her children. She adds nothing to the sum of human spiritual experience, but passes on her potentiality to the next generation. . . . She is sister to the servant of the One Talent, on whose head the wrath of the Master fell.

Nevertheless Erda smiles upon her, infinitely patient, infinitely content.

LAWRENCE

& *APOCALYPSE*

(William Heinemann, Ltd.,
London, 1933)

FOREWORD

THE late D. H. Lawrence and the writer were col-
leagues and friends as elementary school teachers in
Croydon. Their association, beginning in 1909, termi-
nated in 1912, when Lawrence left Croydon.

This little book is partly of the nature of a deferred
conversation.

My acknowledgements are due to Mr. Martin Secker
for permission to print extensively from *Apocalypse*
by D. H. Lawrence.

Holy, holy, holy, Lord God Almighty, which was, and is, and is to come. Out among the stars the Beasts that "rest not day and night" chant eternally. I, sharing their unrest, hear the rhythm of the chant throbbing within me—it must be within me, for my mother has closed the window of the bedroom and drawn blinds and curtains.

Sunday night! Sunday is God's day, standing between two dull stretches of weekday time like a little hill between two lengths of level road. Sunday begins on Saturday evening with the hot bath before the kitchen fire. In the morning there is white underclothing to wear, with embroidery starched at knees and neck, very uncomfortable; but I know the garb of holiness is always stiff and white, from the days of the Angel who expelled Adam and Eve to those of the Redeemed in Revelations— In the chapel, which is the House of God, sunlight comes dim through small coloured panes, staining one's white frock rose and blue. God is conveyed to my perception by the singing, the silences, the minister's oratorical tone, the presence of the great Book. Morning service leads up the hill of Sunday; continuing past the stage of white-glossed and silver-plated dinner one reaches its crown, sometimes inadvertently, sometimes keenly aware. Tall poplars may stress it, pointing pencilled tops to a blue-and-silver heaven; it may be indicated by a quiet wind carrying the rustle of leaves and the resonance of a distant bell, or by the shadow of woods along a remote horizon—things that have no part in weekday consciousness, but belong to God— So, towards late afternoon, one begins to descend; again, at evening, there is the chapel, now warm and secretive, hiding in the night that closes black upon its windows. Inside, people whisper to one another, but "unite," as the minister says, in singing, and become a single voice potent to compel the Presence— Naked gas flames, like luminous evening primroses, yellow the minister's face as he stands in the pulpit behind the Book.

> "Holy, holy, holy, Lord God Almighty!
> Early in the morning our song shall rise to Thee."

The whole content of Sunday's hours passes before me, going up to God for approval or condemnation.

> "Holy, holy, holy, though the darkness hide Thee,
> Though the eye of sinful man Thy glory may not see . . ."

God is becoming unendurably great. The chapel shrinks, the small yellow flames dim and dim, the people are only denser shadows than those flattened on the walls. Cowering, I turn from Sunday, and try to hide among the things of the weekday world. *Sums*—long division sums—things one can *do*—things submissive to the dwindling Something which is I. Grains of commonplace for one's tiny self to cling to— But the preacher's voice, now rising alone into the silence which absorbed the hymn, most mercilessly encourages the overpowering God. Of Him is created a gigantic angel, bearing a great book with seven clasps, and behind the angel a strange Lamb more huge and fearsome than a lion, whose golden fleece hangs in long curls, shining.

*And I beheld, and I heard the voice of many angels round about the
throne and the beasts and the elders; and the number of them was ten
thousand times ten thousand, and thousands of thousands; saying with
a loud voice. "Worthy is the Lamb that was slain to receive power and
riches, and wisdom, and strength, and honour and glory and blessing."*

*And every creature which is in heaven, and on the earth, and under
the earth, and such as are in the sea heard I saying, "Blessing, and
honour, and glory, and power be unto him that sitteth upon the throne
and unto the Lamb, for ever and ever."*

A pæan to shake the universe of an eight-year-old child, sounding through a suddenly-opened door of the ages. The door closes
again; but on the way home from chapel one walks below myriad
stars, and knows that the voices of the Four Beasts are still chant-
ing, like sea-surge far off. Soft, unceasing, beneath the chatter of
home and the business of Sunday supper their song persists,
loudening when the house is quiet, and Sunday drifts away on a
half-sleep.

So, against this work of David Herbert Lawrence's beats the
echo of my first impression of the imagery of the *Apocalypse.*
Succeeding it a memory less remote intrudes, relating to David
himself when he and I taught in school, and wandered our weekends over the Surrey hills, gathering primroses or blackberries in
season, but always the herb philosophy— On an autumn Sunday
evening we come through fir-woods to the brow of a steep slope
above the village of Addington. The wood smoke spirals in
the autumn damp, the church bell tings; along the valley road
villagers are passing to evening service— Shall we go to church?
asks D.—do I want to go to church? It is past sunset, the woods
are all too chill, the church is warm, and we both like singing the
evening hymns—so we go down into the deeper dusk of the
village, drawn to the glow of the church's windows like moths
out of the wood. "You know," says D. seriously, as we go, "when

I'm middle-aged, I shall probably be married and settled, and take my family to church every Sunday— Best so—"

But I feel that for me there can be no final descent into the valley, no rooting in any community. Grateful for evening shelter, I shall make my way in the morning over the next ridge. *Gerade aus.* And D. also, I think, but each of us alone. It was not I who wrote: "*Nous autres,* we touch, but we never repose."

Thus it was. We touched, and parted, and went separately for eighteen years. In the eighteenth year David died, they say. Either I have not yet learned, or have forgotten, what such death signifies to him who suffers it. We knew so well, he and I, the subtler manifestations of death, and intermingling of the potencies of disintegration and growth. We knew that we died and were born daily, our days having an individual measure. But he was ever willing, as I reluctant, to forget yesterday.

And now that I would consider this commentary of Lawrence's on the *Apocalypse,* David stands much in the way of the first chapter. *His* first memories of the *Book of Revelation* are associated with "the strange marvellous black nights of the North Midlands." The soft blackness of the near distance, the sudden white intensity outlining the giant's castle of an iron foundry as molten metal poured from its blast-furnaces, the vibrant pulsing of hidden pit-engines—these, when I came to them, were significant of David. Out of such a world of strange vitalities he appeared to me, who was caught in suburban backwaters; came breaking down reeds, showing the way of escape— I tolerated, wondered, marvelled presently at the deeps below my hand, pushed forth, set sail again—

There was a man sent from God, whose name was—

But this is the beginning of another book than *Apocalypse.* John of Patmos, to Lawrence's mind, was no divine messenger.

This essay upon *Revelation* sets aside those heroic values claimed for the Book ever since its inclusion in the New Testament canon. Its *taboo* is removed, and it is given merely a place—and not too high a place—among the classic allegories. Within the precincts of the *Apocalypse* Lawrence plays *Tytyl* in the Palace of Night. Out come all the mysteries that have terrified the centuries— Plagues and Woes and Vials of Wrath. We must see, says this Tytyl, of what these bogies are made, and from whence they derive. And when he has freed them they are far less impressive than when our imagination conceived them behind the closed doors of priestly traditions.

If that were all, we should have, perhaps, little to thank Lawrence for. In Mystery there is eternal fascination. It is our earnest of infinity, and we cannot be satisfied with less than the infinite. We are children of the Search, and we must be assured that there are yet undiscovered regions. "Behold, I show you a mystery!"— what pronouncement could please us more? The Mystery—not its elucidation. The Seen and the Known imprison us; we must escape into the unfathomed. We will dip our hands into no pool so shallow that our fingers stir the mud at the bottom.

But there are small and great mysteries. The *Apocalypse* terrified Christendom with Plagues and Woes, Vials of Wrath and Desolations, all of which are minor ones. Obsessed by these, we remained unaware of the Palace of Night wherein they found temporary place. To the perception of this Great Mystery, Lawrence brings us. By this leading we know the Buddhas—they expose to the test of common daylight crude little mysteries that we feared, and discover to us the Great Mystery which contained them. In its contemplation there is awe, but not fear.

Let us consider, says Lawrence, the ancient Mystery that lies behind the *Apocalypse*—the background against which its fantastic beasts and angels disport themselves. What are the origins of this allegory—

But here he pauses to say that he hates allegory, and always has hated it:

> I never could read *Pilgrim's Progress*. When, as a small boy, I learnt from Euclid that "The whole is greater than the part" I immediately knew that that solved the problem of allegory for me. A man is more than mere Faithfulness and Truth [he is referring to the horsemen in Rev. 19] and when people are mere personifications of qualities they cease to be people for me.

This is provocative. And I dare say there is much more in D.'s book that he and I shall want to argue about. We might go and sit under the big yew-tree rooted in the slope of a Surrey hill just below our larch-wood. The larch-wood is a ghost—its trees came down during the War—but the yew will shelter the discussions of many starry nights— There is a noiseless white owl that glides luminous, like a blob of moonshine.

H: I don't think I could read *Pilgrim's Progress* now. But when I was seven it was real enough. It seemed silly that the people of the book hadn't proper names, instead of long labels, but they were none the less people. I just ignored the labels.

D: As you ignore everything that doesn't please you. Of course! Then *P.P.* was never allegory to you. It was sheer romance.

H: No! not that. Something more concrete. Something like a geography book, describing places I'd seen. Especially the Delectable Mountains and the River.

D: With the people quite incidental to the landscape. Well! that wasn't allegory. And how about *Revelation?*

H: Probably that wasn't allegory either. The man on the white horse didn't represent Faithfulness and Truth to me any the more because his author said his name was *Faithful and True*. But neither was he real. Rather like a painting hung too high to see properly. But at fifteen I read Olive Schreiner's allegory *The Hunter*——

D: And thought it inspired. You *would* love allegory. You know
   you're always taking bundles of qualities and making images
   of them—pretending they're people. Instead of looking to
   see what real people are made of. That's *you.*
H: Let's come back to the *Apocalypse.*

II

Lawrence finds in the *Book of Revelation* the voice and expression of popular religion. The religion of the uneducated,
unintelligent, powerless, but envious poor. The ruling passion of
this class, he says, is envy, and from it springs the desire to "bring
your grand enemies down to utter destruction and discomfiture,
while you yourself rise up to grandeur." Imaginatively, this is
what the Salvation Army does when it raves at the street corner
about "the Blood of the Lamb, and Babylon, Sion, and Sinners,
the great harlot, and angels that cry Woe! Woe!! Woe!!! and
vials that pour out horrible plagues. And above all about being
Saved, and reigning in Glory, and living in a grand city made of
Jasper with gates of pearl!"
  This may be. But I think it is not the whole truth of the matter;
it does not account fully for the book's appeal to people of to-
day. No doubt the Christian communities of the later first century
A.D. welcomed its outspoken denunciations of the persecuting
power. Such diatribes would have provided relief when the doctrine of non-resistance, at the beginning such a new, pure form
of heroism, had lost the force of novelty and become a little
hackneyed. Then the voice of pride spoke again. The Christian
community spirit began to exult in its isolation, its "otherness,"
its unity in the face of the common enemy, its unique deity and
its immortal destiny. It was satisfying to have Jesus, the meek
and lowly of heart, the Lamb sacrificed for the sin of the elect,
presented in the guise of a glorious and terrifying god, out for
vengeance on the persecutors of his devotees. There were prob-

ably few Christians who found insuperable difficulty in accepting the transformation. The epistles and gospels had provided steps towards this apotheosis; there were the stories of the Transfiguration and Ascension; there was the shining Christ of Paul's vision. The speedy return of the Leader, and the translation of the faithful to the joys of a newly-created heaven were fundamental doctrines of the apostles. And in the Christ of the Second Coming there was not much left of the spirit of the Teacher of Galilee.

Curiously, inevitably, every conception and idea is modified according to the shape and nature of the mind into which it falls. Infinite are the gradations of quality exhibited by the mind of man. "Down among the uneducated people," says D., "you will still find *Revelation* rampant." Like the majority of generalisations, this is misleading. He might more justly have said "among the uneducable people." For in the approach to the book perception is involved as much as, if not more than, education.

Among first-century Christians there were minds of fine and subtle perception, and minds too coarse or stupid to apprehend any but materialistic values; and between these two extremes we can place all the fine shades of mental quality, of emotional, intuitional and imaginative bias. Christianity had to be extraordinarily adaptable to satisfy them all. And it *was*—amazingly adaptable. In our own time mental variations are presumably even more numerous and complex; and between the Christianity of Dean Inge and that of Mrs. Aimée McPherson there is indeed a great gulf fixed. Yet the *Book of Revelation* is probably not without its appeal to many an Anglican of culture.

(Here David breaks in. I wonder, indeed, that he has been quiescent so long.)

D: You're confusing the nature and content of the book itself with the beauty of its translation. *That,* of course, makes an appeal to the man who appreciates good English. Grotius says that its Greek was bad—mixed up with solecisms and foreign words. You can see something of what *Revelation* owes to the excellence of Elizabethan diction if you compare the Authorised Version with the one I've used—Moffatt's. But do you mean to say you think that the *Salvationist* gets excited over beauty of phrase?

H: No! *He* has the sort of child mind that is fascinated by big masses of crude colour. Did you see that exhibition of Brazilian art at the Tate Gallery recently? Scarlet robes, scarlet flesh, bleeding victims—every picture smeared and blotched with red. The Salvationist imagination delights in that kind of thing—and *gilt*. So all the blood and shine of *Revelation* enraptures him. I expect we all pass through that phase sooner or later. I did. I remember at five years of age marching up and down in a perfect ecstasy, shouting:

> "Hallelujah, 'tis done!
> I believe on the Son,
> I am saved by the blood of the crucified one."

D: (he chuckles) *You* as a Mithraist! *Mein Gott!* Well, it's Mithras for the Roman soldier and the Salvationist, anyway—or Mithraism and Yahwehism mixed, thinned down to a syrupy imaginative essence.

H: I think that's more the stimulant than any passion of class resentment.

(D. thrusts both hands suddenly through his thick fair hair, ruffling it furiously, jabs them into his pockets, leans back against the tree-trunk, staring before him with narrowed eyes. His face is white and opaque in its dark shadow. I, looking too closely at him, lose him.)

The book passes from a discussion of *Revelation* as an expression of democratic Christianity to a consideration of the essential differences between aristocrats and democrats:

There's no getting away from it, mankind falls forever into the two divisions of aristocrats and democrats. The purest aristocrats during the Christian era have taught democracy. And the purest democrats try to turn themselves into the most absolute aristocracy. Jesus was an aristocrat, so was John the Apostle, and Paul. It takes a great aristocrat to be capable of great tenderness and gentleness and unselfishness; the tenderness and gentleness of *strength*. From the democrat you may often get the tenderness and gentleness of weakness; that's another thing. But you usually get a sense of toughness.

We are speaking now not of political parties, but of the two kinds of human nature; those that feel themselves strong in their souls, and those that feel themselves weak. Jesus and Paul and the greater John felt themselves strong. John of Patmos felt himself weak, in his very soul.

Is there anyone—has there ever been anyone—who feels or has felt "strong in his soul" *all* the time? Jesus did not. Faced with the imminent prospect of physical agony and death he felt nearly overwhelmed. But he knew also that he *could not* compromise to avoid the issue to which his life had led. *Noblesse oblige.* That is the compulsion of the pure aristocrat. Not my class, not my clan is my judge. *I* only, inexorable—there is no appeal from myself. Whereas the pure democrat finds his ultimate sanction in the popular judgment. He is at peace when he feels that his aims, his desires, his emotions are at one with those of his kind, that his actions are furthering the common good. The aristocrat is his natural antagonist, because, measured by his standards, the aristocrat is an outlaw.

Both aristocrats and democrats were to be found among the early Christians as among their pagan opponents. Both are represented in modern communities. But the democrats, as Lawrence says, were and are in the majority, far outnumbering the aristocrats. It is going too far to say that this will always be so.

. . . the Christian religion became dual. The religion of the strong taught renunciation and love. And the religion of the weak taught *down with the strong and powerful and let the poor be glorified.*

Yes! but it was not the power of an aristocracy that tyrannised over the early Christian communities. The tyranny was that of a larger, more powerful democracy over a smaller. The Christian democracy felt itself subordinate to the pagan democracy. It wanted to get even with the tyrant power. In every material sense it was powerless, poor, unfree. Now the mind of man cannot accept these conditions; it *must* make an attempt at adjustment. If the will works in conjunction with the mind, there is outward and actual rebellion, but if the will is feeble, weakened by the habit of submission or other cause, the imagination usurps its place, and the adjustment is an imaginary one. Hence the popular demand for the novel which offers its reader the opportunity of identifying himself for the moment with the rich, the successful, the daring; which permits him to attain imaginatively any kind of freedom he desires, but is too fearful or too weak to achieve in actuality.

The *Book of Revelation* was the grand effort of first-century Christian imagination. It marked the beginning of a vogue in visions. Its inclusion among the sacred books established the prestige of the visionary and justified the abnegation of effort. The present was to be discounted, the future glorified. To-day you suffer, to-morrow you shall reign. This was the anæsthetic that lulled the Church through early agonies, and sustained the Christianised Empire when it fell into the hands of Goth and Hun. Too useful a drug, it was to be renounced later, when the Church had grown into the strongest, most fully organised power Europe had ever known, with a firmly established authority over the souls of men, and no small claim upon their temporal possessions. But mark the difference in application! Highly creditable was it now to be poor, weak, impotent—even filthy—so much so that lordly prelates paid lip-service to poverty, and on occasion washed the feet of beggars to demonstrate their own humility. For wherein lay the assurance of authority and wealth save in the domination of many humble? And did not a compensatory hereafter divert the imagination from inconvenient enquiry into the nature of the evils of mortal life, so full of oppressions that the Church desired neither to lift nor remedy?

This "religion of the weak" thus implanted, and harrowed into the Western mind for twenty centuries, comes to the democracy of to-day as a mental heritage. It still serves its purpose and supplies an emotional outlet, though in lesser degree. The down-at-heels, the out-of-works, the poor in possessions and in spirit, find warmth and stimulus in the gospel of the Revelation. Unobtrusively they slip into the company of the redeemed, and feel themselves glorified. *"These are they which came out of great tribulation, and have washed their robes, and made them white in the blood of the Lamb. . . . Therefore are they before the throne of God . . . they shall hunger no more."*

But the shouting ceases with Sunday. The doors of the Bethels are closed during the week. "Spiritual experience" is succeeded by "endurance." Endurance is now the Christian term for inertia.

III

Lawrence says:

Just as inevitably as Jesus had to have a Judas Iscariot among his disciples, so did there have to be a *Revelation* in the New Testament . . . Why? . . . Because the nature of man demands it and always will demand it. . . . The Christianity of Jesus applies to a part of our nature only. There is a big part to which it does not apply. And to this part, as the Salvation Army will show you, *Revelation* does apply.

The religions of renunciation, meditation and self-knowledge are for

individuals alone. . . . They express the individual side of man's nature. They isolate this side of his nature. And they cut off the other
side . . . the collective side. The lowest stratum of society is always
non-individual, so look there for the other manifestation of religion.

The religions of renunciation, like Buddhism or Christianity, are
for aristocrats, aristocrats of the spirit. The aristocrats of the spirit are
to find their fulfilment in self-realisation and in service. Serve the
poor! Well and good! But whom are the poor going to serve? It is the
grand question. And John of Patmos answers it. The poor are going
to serve themselves and attend to their own glorification. And by the
poor we don't mean the indigent only; we mean the merely collective
souls, terribly 'middling,' who have no aristocratic singleness and
aloneness. . . . The vast mass are these middling souls.

Well, well! Perhaps they are! It seems to be a terribly middling
world at the present time. Suffering from a bad shortage of aristocrats. There are not nearly enough aristocrats, it would appear,
to go round. Not leaven enough to leaven the lump.

Can anything be done about it? Where do aristocrats come
from? How are they produced? Are they pedigreed souls, aristocrats from the womb? Or is there virtue in the influence of an
aristocratic tradition?

One thing is certain. No amount of wealth ever purchased aristocracy of soul. It may not be impossible for a millionaire to be
an aristocrat, or for an aristocrat to become a millionaire—though
the latter is unlikely. But in our thinking we must keep aristocracy, and wealth (together with the influence it exerts) apart.
There is no relationship between the two. Jesus knew this, and
taught it; but thanks chiefly to the Church, the Western world has
pretty nearly forgotten it.

I submit that both aristocrat and democrat are quick in the soul
of every babe. Their struggle for supremacy begins at birth. It is
an uneven struggle; there is an inherited bias in favour of the one
or the other. Yet the issue is most uncertain. Environment, edu-

cation, human contacts, the sequence of events, the type of equi-
librium maintained by the balance of the mental and emotional
powers—all these influences severally strengthen the one and
weaken the other of the combatants. Sooner or later ascendancy is
decided; the victor is enthroned. Then the vanquished becomes
the rebel, more or less impotent, but still present; a disturbing
possibility, perhaps a voice from the dungeon, speaking at inter-
vals between long silences. But never in the lifetime can the rebel
be expelled finally from the kingdom.

The individual aristocrat is he in whom the qualities of aristocracy are dominant; the individual democrat is he in whom the
qualities of democracy are dominant. The resultant of the forces
exercised by the aristocrat is Power; the resultant of those exercised by the democrat is Resistance.

As soon as two or three men come together especially to *do* something then power comes into being and one man is a leader, a master.
It is inevitable.

Accept it, recognise the natural power in the man, as men did in the
past, and give it homage, then there is a great joy, an uplifting, and a
potency passes from the powerful to the less powerful. There is a
stream of power. And in this men have their best collective being, now
and for ever. Give homage to a hero, and you become yourself heroic
—it is the law of men.

Here is good common sense, and what seems simple direction.
But it is not really as simple as it sounds; two difficulties compli-
cate it. One is the democrat's difficulty in recognising this "natural power"—of distinguishing between the true aristocrat and
the mere boss. The other lies in the fact that the homage of men
imposes upon the aristocratic balance of the leader its severest
testing—and it may fail. The test is threefold. Can he return to
those who thus tender him homage and allegiance their spiritual
freedom unimpaired? Does his touch upon them strengthen the

aristocrat within them? And finally, Can he thus unite with others in a state of collective being, and yet retain the poise and aloofness and integrity of his own soul?

In the "stream of power" how many leaders lose their footing? And in how many more does the energy which should vitalise the group into a unit of creative activity lose its potency and become the mere expression of a tyranny!

But act on the reverse, and what happens? Deny power, and power wanes. Deny power in a greater man, and you have no power in yourself.

This is essentially true. And the majority of people *do* deny power, preferring to accept, sullenly or slavishly, the binding of authority.

Why?

Because authority in itself is dead. It can be measured, parcelled, bestowed. It is limitable, temporary. Resistance can affect its scope, or even overthrow it. But power is the evidence of a living spirit which cannot be expressed in finite terms nor confined within given bounds. It may be weakened, rendered ineffective by denial, strengthened by recognition. In face of power, resistance is uncertain of its weapons.

The individual democrat, lacking faith in himself, is afraid of power in another. If I yield to my leader in a splendid self-abnegation of hero-worship, shall I not lose my own measure of freedom, small as it is? In the past, it is true, disciples have betrayed their masters; but how many more masters have betrayed their disciples? How shall I know him, the true aristocrat, the lord of my soul?

It would be so easy if the mark of the true aristocrat were always evident. If he wore it like the Brahmin his triple thread. Or if he could produce, on demand, his certificate of merit. But such a certificate would be out of date as soon as written, and there is no known sign. The servants of God are not "sealed in their foreheads." And those who go about proclaiming "I am Christ" are pretty certain to be bosses.

And yet power calls to power, truth to truth, as falsehood to falsehood. And he in whom aristocracy is most potent is least likely to mistake or neglect his true leader. Whether or no he will yield allegiance depends on the balance between his aristocratic and democratic selves.

And the collective self either lives and moves and has its being in a full relationship of power; or it is reserved, and lives in a frictional misery of trying to destroy power and destroy itself.

Again, indubitably true. David and I have been wonderfully concordant, so far, in this chapter. But I see serious dissensions approaching.

But nowadays the will to destroy power is paramount. Great kings like the late Tzar—we mean great in position—are rendered almost imbecile by the vast anti-will of the masses, the will to negate power. Modern kings are negated till they become almost idiots. How can the anti-power masses, above all the great middling masses, ever have a king who is more than a thing of ridicule and pathos?

H: Look here, D.—this about the late Tzar is sheer nonsense! And the editorial "we"—I don't like it. I like you much better when you say *I*.

D: Oh—cut out the "we"! Yes, cut it out! I don't like it—it slipped in. But what's the matter with the Tzar? Here! give me the page! [He snatches it and reads it through, frowning.] Well! what is your objection? Can you deny the imbecility? Or its cause?

H: Its cause. Nicholas's feeble-mindedness was no more due to the "anti-will of the masses" than that of any other unfortunate of his kind. That about the negation of modern kings may be true—

D: It *is*—

H: But it's their own acquiescence in the process that affects them personally. They consent to be a shadow-show, to please people who demand a semblance of power while denying it in actuality. "We are figureheads, we are symbols," they say grandly. The admission must conduce to a queer state of mind, a kind of lunacy, but not idiocy. Then, with reference to your next sentence—kings, nowadays, are anachronisms, and as such are bound to be ridiculous, or pathetic, or both.

D: For heaven's sake don't hold forth, H.! That's my job. Yours is to suggest and criticise. Now this about Judas is true, isn't it?

(We read the following passage together.)

Judas had to betray Jesus to the powers that be, because of the denial and subterfuge inherent in Jesus's teaching. Jesus took up the position of the pure individual, even with his disciples. He did not *really* mix with them, or even work or act with them. *He was alone all the time.* He puzzled them utterly, and in some part of them he let them down. He refused to be their physical power-lord. The power-homage in a man like Judas felt itself betrayed! So it betrayed back again—with a kiss. And in the same way, *Revelation* had to be included in the New Testament, to give the death kiss to the Gospels.

H: Yes! I understand, but perhaps not many people will. One might write a play called *The Justification of Judas*—

IV

Lawrence charges the early Christian community with having "a will to destroy all power," and to usurp themselves the final ultimate power.

John of Patmos attributed final, ultimate power to his own deity. I cannot find that he allocated any important part of it to the community. Communal or mass rule is not foreshadowed in the *Book of Revelation*. Certainly there are twenty-four crowned elders seated round the throne of God who declare themselves kings and priests appointed to rule the earth. But they resemble rather the court officials of an Oriental king than the members of a Soviet. They are representatives of the old Jewish priestly hierarchy, with a function of worship preceding that of authority. The "ultimate power" is superhuman power.

That which actually emerged from the democratic early Christian communities was a powerful aristocracy. The Fathers of the Church. The Clements and Cyrils and Augustines and Jeromes. A wonderful succession of them, up to Gregory the Great and Hildebrand. The rule of the Church they established was not communal rule, but again that of the priestly hierarchy. This aristocracy planned, directed, and carried out the civilising of the new, raw, pagan peoples who had seized upon the old Roman Empire. With a proud assumption of spiritual authority it made adopted sons of the victor chiefs, and by diplomacy, cajolery, and threats of divine wrath linked their temporal power to its own. Then its vitality passed away, and what remained was the dead hand of its sanction and authority, in dogma and creed and rule.

After the crash of the Dark Ages, the Catholic Church emerged again a human thing, adjusted to seed-time and harvest and the solstices of Christmas and Midsummer, and having a good balance, in early days, between brotherly love and natural lordship and splendour. Every man was given his little kingdom in marriage, and every woman her little inviolate realm. This Christian marriage guided by the Church was a great institution for true freedom, true possibility of fulfilment. Freedom was no more, and can be no more, than the possibility of living fully and satisfactorily. In marriage, in the great natural cycle of church ritual and festival, the early Catholic Church tried to give this to men.

Here is speaking the David Lawrence who stood with me in the

Helen Corke (1903)

Jessie Chambers (c. 1907)

The Breach, Eastwood, Nottinghamshire, miner's housing where D. H. Lawrence lived, the "Bottoms" of *Sons and Lovers*. The Haggs Farm, Jessie Chambers' home, is just beyond the ridge at the right.

Moorgreen Colliery and Lyncroft Road from Walker Street, Eastwood, Nottinghamshire, showing the Lawrence Country beyond.

No. 12 Colworth Road, Croydon, where Lawrence lodged, 1908–1912.

Davidson Road Boys' School, Croydon, where Lawrence taught, September, 1908–December, 1911.

The Haggs, the Chambers' farm near Eastwood, Nottinghamshire.

Moorgreen Reservoir, the "Nethermere" of *The White Peacock*.

Felley Mill Pond, the "Strelley Mill" of *The White Peacock*.

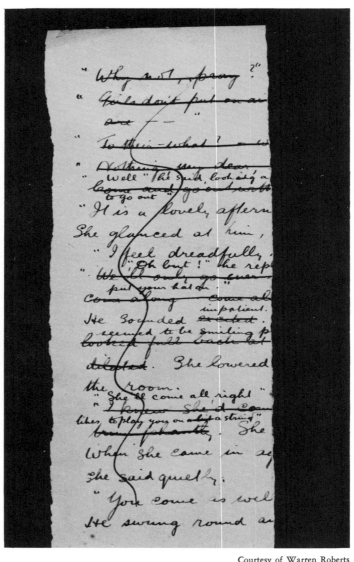

Courtesy of Warren Roberts

This is a scrap of D. H. Lawrence's original MSS. of his first
novel THE WHITE PEACOCK.   When revising he tore the discarded
pages in two, longwise, and a few of these, slipped between the
sheets of the final revision, were preserved with it.

Helen Corke,

autumn dusk on the hillside, listening to the call of Addington church bell in the valley, and sensing peace and fulfilment in the sweet, rank evening mist.

H: I can't idealise the medieval Church. But it adapted itself very successfully to certain human and natural rhythms.

D: I don't *want* you to idealise it. Do it justice, that's all! It took men as it found them and made the best of them. It didn't expect men to be saints—it expected them to sin—and it made proper provision against the times when they *did* sin. It spanked them and rewarded them appropriately. It gave them the vivid contrasts they could appreciate, good and evil, heaven and hell, wealth and poverty, feast and fast. Don't you *see* what a fine balance it kept?

H: It was *mothering* them all the time. Very necessary at first, when they were a childish, simple folk. It took over their decisions, told them what to believe and to do, gave them, as you say, highly coloured pictures and strong emotional contrasts. But it discouraged their growing up—put their minds in irons to keep them small. The Reformation didn't change that—it only changed the irons. So to-day we're more or less a race of mental cripples.

D: You *will* stress the mental aspect! But that's relatively unimportant, subject to variation. While the primal physical and emotional needs remain the same from age to age.

H: Do they? Can the physical and emotional needs of people of to-day be satisfied in precisely the same manner as those of the Middle Ages? I doubt it very much. I like your definition of *freedom*, "the possibility of living fully and satisfactorily." But can that be applied to the state of marriage as guided by the Church of the Middle Ages? From the *wife's* point of view?

D: If she enjoyed possession of man, children, and home, I tell
   you she *had* her essential satisfactions. What more could she
   have wanted?

H: Choice in the matter of a husband, perhaps. But I don't know
   —she was saved the trouble of making a decision—at least if
   she were a ward of the Church.

D: The Church found her a husband when there was little chance
   of her finding one for herself.

H: As it found a bull for its cows—but with rather less discrimi-
   nation as to age and condition.

D: (savagely) Well! she could be the Bride of Christ if she
   didn't want the man. You can't say she hadn't a choice. I
   know what your choice would have been.

H: I! Oh, the Middle Ages burnt *me* for a witch. The Church
   discouraged variations in type.

. . . .

With the Reformation, Lawrence says, the old will of the
Christian community to destroy human power and to substitute
the *negative* power of the mass, began again—and is raging to-
day:

In Russia the triumph over worldly power was accomplished, and
the reign of saints set in, with Lenin for the chief saint.

Lenin's rule of saints turned out quite horrible. It has more thou-
shalt-nots than any rule of "Beasts" or emperors. And this is bound
to be so. Any rule of saints must be horrible. Why? Because the nature
of man is not saintly. The primal need—the old pre-Adamic need in
a man's soul is to be, in his own sphere and as far as he can attain it,
master, lord, and splendid one. Every cock can crow on his own muck-
heap, and ruffle gleaming feathers, every peasant could be a glorious
little Tzar in his own hut, and when he got a bit drunk. And every
peasant was consummated in the old dash and splendour of the nobles,
and in the supreme splendour of the Tzar.

No! It's plausible, but it's wrong. You, D. H. L., have not visualised Russia as Lenin did. The majority of Russian peasants were too far away from the stimulating show, too remote in misery from any exhibition of the "dash and gorgeousness of the nobles" and the "supreme splendour of the Tzar," to enjoy this imaginary consummation. Nor did it compensate any who experienced it for the negations and disabilities of serfdom. There *is* a primal need in the soul to achieve, to consolidate, and to go on achieving, which is life; but you have confused it with the desire to possess, to bind, and to go on possessing, which is death. Your peasant, turning from the clumsy hand-share behind which he has hobbled in mud so long, may find more satisfaction in mastery of the giant tractor which ploughs acres as the hand-share ploughed rods, than in an imaginary lordship of Russia. *Peer Gynt* may dance bravely, but he is nevertheless a pathetic figure.

Lenin, the saint, saw the peasant and the artisan trodden by the power of the despot and the power of money into the soil of Russia. They should be placed upon their feet, said he; if inertia bound them they must be dragged out of the mud; and the hills should be levelled and cast into the marshes so there might be firm ground, level ground, for men to walk upon. Russia a fertile plain, whereon men should stand side by side! In the power and by the vision of Lenin this thing is being done. Lenin is dead, but there is a vital challenge and response between him and the Russian people yet. The test of his leadership is not at an end. Will he eventually restore to his followers their spiritual freedom unimpaired? Does his touch upon them strengthen the positive powers of the individual within them? For if these things can be shown there will still be "brave people who add up to an aristocracy" in Russia, and this aristocracy may be one of the most powerful and fruitful the world has ever known.

But Lawrence hates and fears community rule. For him it is "the Beast":

The community is inhuman, and less than human. It becomes at last the most dangerous, because the most bloodless and insentient tyrant. For a long time even a democracy like the American or the Swiss will answer to the call of a hero who is somewhat of a true aristocrat; so strong is the aristocratic instinct in man. But the willingness to give the response to the heroic, the true aristocratic call, gets weaker and weaker in every democracy as time goes on. Then men turn against the heroic appeal. They will only listen to the call of mediocrity wielding the insentient bullying power of mediocrity, which is evil. Hence the success of painfully inferior and even base politicians.

When relating his philosophy to the individual soul, Lawrence made few mistakes. The preceding passage is true for the individual. But since any community in the ordinary sense of the word is the sum of the people who compose it, its government is bound to reflect the *dominant* qualities of its members, whatever those qualities may be. Moreover, circumstances and events of the time will tend to stimulate or depress the more aristocratic qualities. That is to say, a community of relatively mean people will have a mean government, ready to act basely both towards its own supporters and outsiders, yet capable of showing some bravery and generosity when temporarily stimulated by such conditions as those affecting Europe in August, 1914. And a community of relatively generous people will have a government inclined to show a generous spirit both at home and abroad, although such world-wide depression as we are now experiencing (December, 1931) may temporarily debase its standards.

Brave people add up to an aristocracy. The democracy of thou-shalt-not is bound to be a collection of weak men. . . . When the will of the people becomes the sum of the weakness of a multitude of weak men, it is time to make a break.

It is indeed. And the break is inevitable.

So to-day. Society consists of a mass of weak individuals trying to protect themselves, out of fear, from every possible imaginary evil, and, of course, *by their very fear,* bringing the evil into being. This is the Christian community to-day, in its perpetual mean thou-shalt-not. This is how Christian doctrine has worked out in practice.

There is Lawrence's indictment! And every individual in whom the aristocrat lives, every Christian who honours his faith, every democratic community in the Western world, had better question it seriously and examine the evidence from which he draws his conclusions. For if indeed this is all our social legislation and philanthropy amount to, our civilisation is condemned, and sentenced to extinction by spiritual and biological law.

V

We have been wandering long about the precincts of the *Apocalypse.* Now we are going to enter by the gate of the dedication.

Lawrence quotes nearly the whole of the first chapter, using the Moffatt translation, because, he says, it is a little more explicit than the Authorised Version. I think he wants to free the text for himself, as far as possible, from the aura it carried in childhood, and perhaps also from the magic of Elizabethan diction.

The quotation describes the Jesus of *Revelation* "in the midst of the seven lampstands." Comparing this Being with the Jesus of Gethsemane, Lawrence says:

And this is Jesus: not only the Jesus of the early churches, but the Jesus of popular religion to-day. There is nothing humble nor suffering here. And it is a true account of man's *other* conception of God: perhaps the greater and more fundamental conception: the magnificent Mover of the Cosmos. To John of Patmos, the Lord is *Kosmokrator,* even *Kosmodynamos*; the great ruler of the Cosmos and the Power of the Cosmos.

But the Jesus of John's vision is more even than this. He holds the

keys that unlock death and Hades. He is Lord of the Underworld. He
is Hermes, the guide of souls through the death-world, over the hellish
stream. He is master of the mysteries of the dead, he knows the meaning of the holocaust, and has final power over the powers below. The
dead and the lords of death, who are always hovering in the background of religion away down among the people, these Chthonioi of
the primitive Greeks, these, too, must acknowledge Jesus as a supreme
lord.

And the lord of the dead is master of the future and the god of the
present. He gives the vision of what was, and is, and shall be.

What is modern Christianity going to make of it? Modern Pro-
testantism and Christianity alike, cut off from the Cosmos, cut off from
Hades, cut off from the magnificence of the Star-Mover. Petty little
personal salvation, petty morality instead of cosmic splendour. We
have lost the sun and the planets, and the Lord with the seven stars of
the Bear in his right hand. Poor, paltry, creeping little world we live
in, even the keys of death and Hades are lost.

That is a cry of intolerable anguish. But it is the cry of David
Lawrence, not of the modern world. If the modern world has lost
the cosmos it is supremely indifferent to its loss. The planets and
the seven stars of the Bear—they are incidental features of a night
sky banished by the electric light. Anyone interested in such ancient matters must drive into the country, push down lanes or
stumble over meadows with clumsy feet unaided by eyes that cannot focus in darkness—and presently he may see them, the stars,
mere pinpoints in heaven, dim, remote, less magnificent than the
white radiance hovering over the hidden city. But who will make
so aimless a journey? Let the scientists, whose business it is, ob-
serve and analyse the stars! Let them set down the results of their
observations in sufficiently readable books, and if these are well
illustrated we will glance at them in our very limited leisure time.
And possibly we do find the star diagrams amusing, and resolve
to look for the groups when we next go a-hiking; in the mean-
time, to make things homely and comfortable, we change the stars'

outlandish foreign names for those of our pet animals and the "talkie" stars who companion so many of our evenings.

Enough of this. The "terribly middling" souls seem to be worrying me also. Yet I should know that they do not form the modern world's unique population. Like the poor, they have been always with us; they are not the new creation of a mechanical age. Homer and Socrates suffered more at their hands than I am likely to do. Theirs is the ground-bass of the world's music, which I forget when an individual melody rises.

They have not lost the cosmos; they were never aware of it; they never will be. But discerning souls like David Lawrence have lost it, and are plagued in their consciousness on account of such loss, as one becomes aware of bodily health when it is failing. Yet the seven stars of the Bear in the Lord's right hand are still more potent than the nine aeroplanes of a bombing squadron, and the signs of the zodiac are set in a handwriting that will stand distinct when the fashion of sky advertising has passed into the category of barbarisms. The cosmos has not lost us. We are ever the issue of its vitality. As Lawrence admits:

> We and the cosmos are one. The cosmos is a vast living body, of which we are still parts. The sun is a great heart whose tremors run through our smallest veins. The moon is a great gleaming nerve centre from which we quiver forever. If we get out of contact and harmony with the sun and moon, then both turn into dragons of destruction. The sun is a great source of blood-vitality, it streams strength to us. But once we resist the sun, and say: It is a mere ball of gas!—then the very streaming vitality turns into a subtle disintegrative force in us and undoes us. The same with the moon, the planets, the great stars.

We, being human, can best establish this harmony through human contacts. For some of us there is no other way. It was David Lawrence who showed me this, twenty-three years ago, when death had broken the most vital contact I had formed, up to that date, with my kind. The breaking of that great circuit had dis-

connected all the slighter, more impersonal contacts, and I knew
nothingness, conceiving the universe as a vast negation. The sun
was indeed "a mere ball of gas," and violin-playing the scraping
of hairs upon catgut. For two years Lawrence, the engineer,
worked to establish a new connection, tried to restore Helios to
me, to show me Isis living, Isis in search. The contacts he helped
me to form have grown stronger with the passing of years—I
doubt if catastrophe could break them now. But when I hear him
cry, "We have lost the cosmos—even the keys of death and Hades
are lost!" it is like an echo of that earlier cry, *Eloi, eloi, lama sa-*
bachthani. Sometimes there is nothing to do but wait till the earth
has finished trembling.

VI

Lawrence believed that we have "lost the cosmos." That is to
say, we have no longer any persuasion, mental or emotional, of
our unity with the infinite. We are no longer "members of one
body" working together in unconscious rhythm, but disintegrate,
each of us striving blindly and stupidly for a destructive individual consciousness. Thus:

The cosmos became anathema to the Protestants after the Reformation. They substituted the non-vital universe of forces and mechanistic
order; everything else became abstraction, and the long, slow death of
the human being set in. This slow death produced science and ma-
chinery, but both are death-products. It . . . will end in the annihilation of the human race unless there is a change, a resurrection, a return
to the cosmos.

Here is perversity! D. H. L. refusing, with the churchmen of
Galileo's day, to look through the telescope, and reproving Coper-
nicus and Tycho Brahe for discarding astrology in favour of as-
tronomy. Telling the scientist that he is poisoning the race with
apples from the tree of knowledge. There is more intuition in the
phrase of Emerson: *"In a centred mind, it matters nothing how*

many mechanical inventions you exhibit. Nature adopts them very fast into her vital circles, and the gliding train of cars she loves like her own." But D. H. L. qualifies his statement, showing a little diffidence. "No doubt," says he, "the death was necessary." When we read a sentence beginning "No doubt," we may reasonably assume doubts on the part of the writer.

I don't believe in this "long, slow death of the human being," supposed by Lawrence to have set in after the Reformation. Not the withdrawal or extinction of life. Perhaps a slow disintegration began then. A process of division, a splitting away, a schism, a change. With the fifteenth century we entered upon an analytical phase of human development. We wanted to examine, to separate, to define, to discover.

The Church got nervous and angry. What was to happen to the nice tight little universe it had conceived and taught? Heaven, Purgatory, Hell—and Earth as a sort of feeding-box for supplying them all. It took up the attitude of John of Patmos, and prepared to curse any who should add to or subtract from its approved conception of the cosmos. But that did not prevent Newton from discovering and enunciating the laws of gravity, nor, after Newton, the spate of scientific thought and its application which flung us To-day.

> Change and decay in all around I see—
> O Thou who changest not, abide with me!

That is the deathly attitude. *Rigor mortis*—the state of life withdrawn.

Change is not death. The cosmos, that binds, can loose also. It hurled the planets from the sun, demanding of them a separate existence, as by cell-division it determines the diverse organs in the body of the unborn. It flings the individual from the group, decreeing him a new orbit, and fulfilment only in isolation.

But man, if he cannot *lose* what he has once known in his very being, can, for a longer or shorter time, forget it. Let us but turn our eyes to Earth, and Earth, like a jealous mother, claims our undivided attention. The Roman Empire, in its materialism, was forgetting the cosmos in the days when John of Patmos was writing the *Book of Revelation*. The firmament was receding, the stars becoming dim. John had to borrow the eyes of men who had lived before him and seen the heavens nearer the earth.

As Lawrence points out, the Jewish apocalyptist was the successor of the Jewish prophet. An apocalyptic writing was always the language of hope deferred. But the Christian Jew of the later first century A.D. had had a double disappointment. The unfulfilled Messiah prophecies, re-interpreted by the apostles with reference to the second coming of Christ, were not justifying their Christian interpretation. Therefore John, or the writers edited by John, seized upon the visions of Ezekiel and Daniel and Zachariah, recast their symbolism, mixed it with apostolic exhortation, and flung the whole with a grand gesture into a spacious and indefinite future. Which process is probably being imitated by feebler apocalyptists at this moment; it certainly was twenty years ago.

In his reading of *Revelation*, Lawrence notes three points. First, the book appears to him to be divided into two discrepant halves, with separate intentions; second, the imagery in these two halves is respectively primarily pagan and primarily Jewish; third, the author makes persistent use of *power-titles*, both for God and for Jesus. Next he comments:

It is one book, in several layers; like layers of civilisation as you dig deeper and deeper to excavate an old city. Down at the bottom is a pagan substratum, probably one of the ancient books of the Ægean civilisation; some sort of a pagan Mystery. This has been written over by Jewish apocalyptists, then extended, and then finally written over by the Jewish-Christian apocalyptist John: and then, after his day,

expurgated and corrected and pruned down and added to by Christian
editors who wanted to make of it a Christian work.

Very queer, very fascinating to consider, is the way in which the
human mind, having adopted and "stabilised," as it were, a conception, will mould on to it other conceptions utterly dissimilar
and remote, without perceiving any incongruity. The central figure of the Christian faith in its earliest phase was the Teacher—
the Master-philosopher, slain by Roman tools of the Jewish priesthood. Bereaved disciples laboured to make a mental reconstruction
of the life they had shared with the Master, and to preserve his
sayings and doings, the image of his personality as they had
known it. That sufficed for a time; it satisfied the human love of
his personal friends. But soon a halo of myth began to crown the
figure of the Teacher. To new converts, the *human* touch was
lacking, and it was necessary to present the teaching as that of a
Master supernaturally impressive. He awoke from the death-
swoon, He ascended into the heaven from which He should soon
return. Behold a second personality! Side by side with the Teacher
of non-resistance, who had bidden his followers turn the other
cheek to the smiter, and who consistently refused to sanction violent opposition to the civil authority arresting him, we have a
figure majestic, of god-like power. The primitive Church found
apparently no difficulty in reconciling the two, of uniting them in
the same person. The truth is that the Jewish mind was simply
hankering after a Power-Figure. The Messiah was over-due—
willy-nilly it *would* have a Messiah in some form. Here was Jesus,
an undoubted individual, a leader of thought, sufficiently impressive to come into conflict with the conservative majority. To the
wisdom His words had shown in life, power and glory might be
added, since, being dead, he could no longer refuse, as He had
refused temporal power, an apotheosis. Being once lifted into the
heavens, there was Jesus, in all the heavenly company that the

Babylonian and Semitic mind had been assembling since Isis bore
her son Horus and Marduk drove in his chariot of winds to battle
with the forces of Tiarmat. And henceforth the Church made it
obligatory for converts to accept both presentations. It was necessary to confess that Jesus was the Christ—if you didn't you would
"without doubt perish everlastingly." Actually, all through the
centuries, men and women have dwelt upon one or the other presentation, according to their individual need. Therefore we can
sing at evening service:

> Come not in terrors as the King of kings,
> But kind and good, with healing in thy
>   wings,
> Tears for all woes, a heart for every plea—

following it by:

> Crown him with many crowns—
> The Lamb upon his throne!
> Hark how the heavenly anthem drowns
> All music but its own—

with placid disregard of any discrepancy.

John of Patmos had no use for the son of woman and brother
of man. His mind was a mirror of the ancient pagan terrors and
splendours, and under his Christian humility his nationalism
raged with thwarted fury against the Roman power. So for him
the Lamb of God becomes a rampant lion of Assyrian type—a
sort of Sennacherib, ready to wreak the extreme of his wrath upon
the City of the Seven Hills.

Lawrence thinks that John of Patmos had first-hand knowledge
of the pagan star-cults. I believe that John's was unconscious
paganism, that, as a good Jew, he would have been scandalised by
the suggestion that his prophet ancestors borrowed their symbolism from Babylon. The Eastern Fathers probably knew more than
he about star-cults; they refused the *Book of Revelation* canonical

right. Fortunately for the work the Western Fathers, with the exception of Jerome, managed to swallow it without great difficulty or ill effects, and thereafter nobody was unwise enough to find anything but orthodox Christianity, legitimate first-century Christianity, in its pages. The medieval churchmen, who shut the door so firmly on pre-Christian knowledge, probably found the Beasts useful—the Bottomless Pit wanted populating; but the Creatures bore little resemblance to the Sphinxes of Heaven when the churchmen had finished with them.

The following are Lawrence's suggestions as to the construction of the *Apocalypse*:

1. The oldest part (a) a description of the ritual of initiation into one of the pagan Mysteries, Artemis or Cybele—east Mediterranean.

2. This book of ritual written over by a Jewish apocalyptist with a view to substituting the Jewish idea of a Messiah and a Jewish salvation for the individual experience of pagan initiation.

3. Writing (b) probably re-written by a Jewish-Christian author who had extended it in the manner of the Book of Daniel to foretell the utter downfall of Rome.

4. Writing (c) re-written by John of Patmos, who invented little, but intensified the passages dealing with the destruction of the Roman power and priesthood.

5. Petty mutilation of the work by later Christian scribes, with intent to cut out the more obviously pagan references.

Here Lawrence's hatred of the Christian intolerance of things pagan, and his indignation at the Church's denial of pre-Christian wisdom and culture lead him to make a long digression.

VII

Even modern science, Lawrence thinks, is unfair to the earlier races.

The strange thing is that even true scholars, who write scholarly and impartial books about the early Greeks, as soon as they mention the autochthonous races of the Mediterranean, or the Egyptians, or the Chaldeans, insist on the childishness of these peoples, their perfectly trivial achievement, their necessary *Urdummheit* . . . Why, in the oldest of peoples, in the Egyptian friezes and the Assyrian, in the Etruscan paintings and the Hindu carvings we see a splendour, a beauty, and very often a joyous sensitive intelligence which is certainly lost in our world of *Neufrechheit*. If it is a question of primal stupidity or new impudence, then give me primal stupidity.

Now it is a difficult and dangerous thing to make generalised comparisons between the intelligence and achievement of the primitive races and of our own. For our civilisation is based upon, and receives the impulse for its shaping, from an inheritance of conscious memory that has been accumulating for more than three thousand years since Egyptian culture began to decline. And inasmuch as the primitive races lacked this conscious memory, their civilisation was raised upon, and sharpened by, an inheritance of instinctive, unconscious memory, such as determines the impulses of children, and persons of undeveloped mind, to-day. Creations of beauty, of joyous sensitive intelligence are common to both forms of civilisation. Who has not seen the drawings of Prof. Cizek's boys and girls? Or the designs of young architects whose joy in creation is yet unspoilt by commercial exploitation? Have any thirty years of any previous civilisation produced so much fine, sensitive verse (I will not say "joyous," since joy was not born of our time) as these of our twentieth century? If the churchmen and the scientists are unjust to the early peoples, surely Lawrence is no less unfair to his own generation!

But why, indeed, should the term *Urdummheit* be applied to primitive races? We don't talk of the "primal stupidity" of a young child. We know, or ought to know, that the child has direct instinctive reactions and a spontaneity of expression that make him more nearly akin to early peoples than to the fully adult folk about him. He has yet to develop the self-consciousness and mental awareness that is the peculiar characteristic of the modern adult mind. But his range of physical sensation is probably wider than ours, and responds to subtler stimuli. We know that experience, for him, is concentrated and focused in a moment of present time, that its light and shadow are determined by vibrations from the past, but that with the future he has no conscious concern. And, unless we are stupid and insensitive ourselves, we do not expect from the child logical processes nor moral concepts.

Ah, but so many of us *have* grown stupid and insensitive, and utterly forgetful of our own child selves. Are not *we* also enclosed within the narrow circle of our present moment? I cannot otherwise account for the unintelligence and rigidity of our educational schemes, and the extraordinary inability of well-intentioned parents to comprehend the nature of a child's reactions to its world. It is not surprising, if our perceptions fall so short in this instance, that few of us can make an approach to the primitive civilisations with senses capable of echoing a response to theirs. *Why* are we so forgetful? So content with the spot-light of consciousness that whitens the little patch of present experience? So complacently certain that nothing beyond its tiny circle matters in comparison with the minutiæ within!

This complacency so irritates Lawrence that he looks with an inflamed eye on the modern world. Looks and finds it lacking in all the excellencies he has discovered in the life of ancient Chaldea, Egypt, Italy, and Crete.

I do not know by what standards he judges. Though, heaven help us! all standards wobble when fierce gusts of irritation blow. But surely our age deserves rather more respect and much more patience than he is willing to grant it. Certainly it possesses in some measure the qualities whose absence he deplores. We cannot lift our virtues and flout them above us like banners, nor, when our pioneers make really breathless discoveries, do we invariably advertise them in the daily press—nor is it for us to frame memorials to the living. We do well to defer judgment. If it is ill-timed to praise, it is also foolish to condemn; Time will put us in our place. In the meanwhile, generalisations upon the characteristics of the present age are apt to tell us more about the mind of their maker than of the minds of his contemporaries.

Culture and civilisation are tested by vital consciousness. Are we more vitally conscious than the Egyptians of 3000 years B.C.?

Our conscious range is wide, but shallow as a sheet of paper. We have no depth of consciousness.

I think this is rather the expression of profound personal need than the result of acute and protracted observation. How often has Lawrence repeated, in varying phrase, "I find an echo to my own deeps in very few souls; I am out of contact . . ."

Well, it is not such an uncommon experience. There is always the crowd with a wider or narrower *conscious* range and a fear of the unknown, both as unplumbed and unexplored. And there are the others, articulate or silent, who are not afraid, but who know their own loneliness. Our age will be judged not according to the manifestations of its herd-soul, but according to the depth and range of the individual consciousness which emerges from and transcends it. I do not doubt that this century is producing souls of fine and profound individual quality, of subtle intuition and foresight, equal in essential knowledge to those of any past age. But many of them hide themselves, half-ashamed of possessions they cannot share.

We have lost almost entirely the great and intricately-developed sensual awareness or sense awareness, and sense-knowledge, of the ancients. It was a great depth of knowledge arrived at directly, by instinct and intuition, as we say, not by reason. It was a knowledge based, not on words, but on images.

True! There have been considerable losses of this kind on the way to A.D. 1932. Even my cat, presumably, lacks some of the instinctive knowledge that served her Syrian ancestor. How much more have I lost! Minna runs securely in the dark, while I must walk with caution; and she is aware of an infinite variety of scents that pass me by unperceived. When she needs her kind, she is visited by males who travel a considerable distance, and who are never seen at other times in the garden. I do not know by what means she communicates with them; they come, they remain three or four days; then they are gone. I can neither call my kind nor recognise by direct sense perception a summons from the absent. Looking back into my childhood I realise that it was haunted by puzzling and sometimes terrifying half-perceptions of lost knowledge; and I have little doubt that this experience is common to most children. Our ancestors of the remote past owed their survival to the free exercise of sense-perceptions which are now no longer indispensable. Many generations inherited but ceased to use them, or denied them; in us they awake but to die before we come to maturity.

Objective knowledge, communicated by words, has too largely replaced that based on intuition, conveyed directly, or by the conception of mental images. Both kinds have their value, but we are making the mistake of overestimating the one and discounting the other. Again, for action prompted by intuition we have substituted *imitative* action. By these means we are impoverishing ourselves, and inasmuch as we frame educational schemes on such mistaken lines, we are denying our children the use of a large part of their inheritance. The printed page is one of the most evilly potent of our false gods. We devote the modern child to it from the fifth year. We goad him into reading; any seven-year-old who has not learned to read knows well that his fellows regard him as an inferior. Henceforth obsession with ready-made images hampers natural creation. The child must wrestle with the conceptions of the adult, though they be ornate, unwieldy, imperfectly comprehended; he must mouth phrases for him without meaning, and sentiments that have no echo in his own emotions. If his individuality is strong he may waste his energy for years in fruitless attempts to reconcile this apparently sacred Word with his own *Real*; if weak, the Word soon triumphs and he stores his memory with the second-hand, the uncomprehended, the formula which, once fixed in mind, puts on sacredness and authority. I would desire no child to read before the age of ten, but to be trained, up to that age, to express itself in speech, simply, exactly and musically. If it wants to read at an earlier age, let it learn, but do not let it fancy that its reading is anything to be proud of. Encourage it to dance and to draw and model, give it pictures and the simpler forms of good music, see that its ear is trained to listen keenly and acutely both to music and speech.

The children must travel the road of the ancients before they arrive at the door of the present era. They should use, naturally, what Lawrence calls the "rotary-image" way of thinking, untrammelled by any obligation to ape logical processes, until such time as the logical faculty begins to develop. It will show itself, sooner or later, in all persons of good average intelligence. But we have become so impatient that we countenance in our schools a great deal of cruelty, sheer stupid cruelty, practised with the object of trying to force its development.

VIII

Man thought, and still thinks, in images. But now our images have hardly any emotional value. We always want a conclusion, an end, we always want to come, in our mental processes, to a decision, a finality, a full-stop. This gives us a sense of satisfaction. All our mental consciousness is a movement onwards . . . Whereas of course there is no goal. Consciousness is an end in itself. We torture ourselves getting somewhere, and when we get there it is nowhere, for there is nowhere to get to.

Is this general, or even common, experience? Or do only Lawrence and such as he, startled by the difference between their natural mode of thought and that of their relatively primitive fellows, protest in this way? The passage leaves me with a sense of confusion. Consciousness, as I know it, is the whole field of mental and emotional awareness; thought is a track definitely made across it. Here, as I sit under the Knole beeches, my field of consciousness includes the perception of a green deep-turfed valley and its further slope, bounded by oak and hornbeam, the mocking warble of blackbirds in the grove behind me, the remote purr of cars on a main road, the varying marbles of a grey-purple sky. The concourse of images and sensations brings its peculiar emotional values, and whenever this moment rises into memory, something of the emotional value will rise with the images. But my *thought* was not engaged with any part of this field of consciousness till stimulated by the impulse to use it in illustration. My thought was concerned with the search to find in my own mind something corresponding to Lawrence's experience as expressed above.

Yet what follows is clear enough: To the ancients

. . . a thought was a completed state of feeling-awareness, a cumulative thing, a deepening thing, in which feeling deepened into feeling in consciousness till there was a sense of fullness. A completed thought was the plumbing of a depth like a whirlpool of emotional awareness, and at the depth of this whirlpool of emotion the resolve formed. . . . As a matter of fact we do very much the same in a crisis. When anything very important is to be decided we withdraw and ponder and ponder until the deep emotions are set working and revolving together, revolving, revolving, till a centre is formed and we "know what to do."

It is profoundly true. In such wise we resolve to marry, or murder—to do those things involving some form of self-immolation. But we have a myriad decisions to make that do not involve our own being so deeply.

Over the decayed, lichened fence beside me hovers a queen wasp. Her handsome striped body is agleam and aquiver, her eyes are black-brilliant jets of light. She settles deftly, rips the soft surface of the decayed wood, rolls it into neat, tight little green balls, tucks them close till she can carry no more. Then away, droning her deep hum, to the nest-building in the hedge. "I ought," say I, first observing her, "to kill the creature. Her brood will feed on my neighbours' plums as they ripen, and attack my Cox's Orange apples." But I do not kill her. She is too much a bit of the bright morning, too vital and vivid. Emotionally, æsthetically I appreciate her—and the issue of my appreciation will be a wasp colony in August, and emotion of another kind when fruit-picking time comes.

Moreover, the primitive kind of mental activity is ineffective when the ensuing action must be *constructive*. By its aid I can call into my consciousness an image, for example, of the garden I desire. There it is, this portion under fruit, this under vegetables, a shrubbery here, peaches upon this wall, clematis clambering over this summer-house. But the garden will begin and end as a mental image unless I bring constructive thought to bear upon the matter. Decisions must be made at every point. How shall this poor soil, too poor to carry fruit with success, be improved; with what quantity of basic slag and natural manure shall it be treated before the trees are planted? By what means shall I drain the water-logged portion conceived as kitchen-garden? Is it worth while to build a wall *so*, running north and south? will peaches ripen with a western aspect? No "rotary-image" method can help me with such decisions—they will be made in accordance with the measure of my previous knowledge, theoretical or practical, and of my power of observation and deduction.

The fact that no politician to-day has the courage to follow this intensive method of "thought" is the reason of the absolute paucity of the political mind to-day.

D., your "fact" is a mere assumption. So I will counter it with a suggestion no less questionable. Mine is:

The fact that no politician to-day is impersonal enough to refrain entirely from this intensive method of "thought" is the reason of the absolute paucity of constructive policy to-day.

(An argument proceeds, leading back eventually to Section IX of the *Apocalypse.*)

IX

D: Tell me what you think of this section!

H: That would take a long time. There's much that to me is indisputably true, strange new truth—and the stuff of a controversy in every other paragraph. By the way—Salvation Army music comes in again. Have you ever realised how much of Revelation is wrapped in music of another class? The old masters of chorus work—Handel and Bach and Spohr? When I glance at the words of the text they lift at once in the great chorales of the oratorios, and I can't dissociate them from the emotional content of the music.

D: Well! but is there much difference between Handel and the Salvation Army? [While *H.* is thinking this out he continues.] There's a common basic brew of emotion—and developing from it two grades of musical art—

H: With an acute difference between the refined and crude grades. But aren't you getting tired of digressions? I am—I want to follow your working out of the apocalyptic plan.

D: *Sehr gut!*

He passes over the book, pulls a blade of grass to chew, and leans against the tree trunk, hands clasped behind his head. I read:

In heaven the Lamb breaks the seals of the scroll, the starry Beasts utter their tremendous Come! . . . the Four Horsemen, one after another, ride in on their white, red, black and "pale" horses, to bear hence the destructive powers loosed upon the universe by the Cosmic Will.

The famous book of seven seals in this place is the body of a man: of Adam: of any man: and the seven seals are the seven centres or gates in his dynamic consciousness. We are witnessing the opening and the conquest of the great psychic centres of the human body. The old Adam is going to be conquered, die, and be reborn as the new Adam: but in stages, in sevenfold stages, or in six stages and then a climax, seven. For man has seven levels of awareness, or seven spheres of consciousness—

I cannot follow those "seven spheres of consciousness." I realise only two spheres, the tribal and the individual, polarised against each other, eternally in opposition. And for the "levels of awareness"—they may be seven or seventy or seven myriads—they merge so imperceptibly that I can number them no more than the tones of colour in the spectrum.

The succeeding passage on the significance of the horse, the horse of the ages, is pure poetry, a delight. Then David's mind leaps to overtake the Four Horsemen. They are, he says, four stages out of seven in a pagan initiation, four phases of self-conquest, self-immolation. These phases past, the initiate has experienced, symbolically, the death of the body and the descent into Hades. In the Underworld he is divested of his two divine natures, soul and spirit. Remains the living *I*, the "stark flame" which, being immortal, rises, clothes itself anew.

Some such form of initiation, derived from ancient Babylonian and Persian ritual, was practised by the Gnostics of the first and second centuries of the Christian era. One is reminded of the Gnostic contribution to the so-called Apostles' Creed: "He descended into hell, and the third day He rose again from the dead." Why does that remain, why has it come down to us through nineteen centuries, when all detail of the initiatory ceremony, with its complexity of elaborate symbolism, has been long forgotten? Because, I think, this single brief statement preserves the essential simplicity of a perfect symbol. Symbols belong to the realm of shadows. A symbol should present us with a stimulating suggestion, not a concrete idea. Its message should be whispered, its form as cloud-shape on the point of dissolution. The Gnostic phrase in the Creed is to me the expression of a rich and potent symbol. But its elaboration into a definite sequence of psychic experiences, numbered and staged, as in this chapter of Lawrence's book, means little or nothing. I am convinced of the reality of these stereotyped human and divine natures, this process of the unrobing and re-robing of the immortal ego. These *selves* are as artificial as the Four Horsemen of Dürer.

Lawrence himself finds the correspondence between the ancient book of ritual and John's *Revelation* breaking down after the opening of the Fourth Seal; and he attributes the disturbance of the symbolic sequence to the alterations of later Christian editors. But the reappearance of the initiated at the conclusion of their ordeal is unmistakably indicated in the text. Here they come! "These are they that came out of great tribulation, and have washed their robes . . . therefore are they before the throne of God and serve Him day and night in His temple!" What can it be but the annunciation of the "new-born" to the waiting crowds in the temple court?

This vivid scene of the glorification of a new initiate and his identification or assimilation to the god, amid grand brilliance and wonder, and the sound of flutes and the swaying of garlands, was, as we know, the end of the ritual of the mysteries of Isis. Such a scene has been turned by the apocalyptist into a Christian vision.

There are probably many people who can remember how the ancient immortal ecstasy rippled their childish consciousness. I have no more vivid recollection of childish emotional experience than of that which came to me at the age of eight or nine, singing, on Easter Day, in chapel, "The strife is o'er, the battle done—"

> The powers of death have done their worst,
> And Jesus hath His foes dispersed—
> Let songs of joy and triumph burst,
>   Alleluia!

It was not the impression of a crucified and risen Christ that thrilled me. It was no vision of a figure, divine or human—only a *feeling* of white garments in sunlight, of waving shadows, of immeasurable, wonderful gladness. A primitive immortal ecstasy which passed and could not be recaptured to cage in thought; passed like a flash of dragon-fly wings in the rainbow spray of a torrent, to surprise me again at higher levels.

X

After the great climax of the initiation, "there was silence in heaven about the space of half-an-hour."

John of Patmos, we must admit, has artistic instinct, feeling for essential rhythm. More indeed than we, with our crass modern demand that "life, death, and the vast forever" shall be "one grand sweet song"; with our loud-speaker approximation to this achievement. With our yearning for cocktail brilliance, our tendency to exploit to the utmost our emotional and intellectual capacity, our shout of "Oh, well run, sir! keep it up!" to each latest exhibition of literary agility. Some of us would deny the very lark's desire to flutter down, silent, to its home meadow, and be ready to applaud a record-breaking performance on the part of the bird that would leave it with a cracked throat. How we worry ourselves to *do* more and more—or we must *feel*—we get badly scared if our sensibility appears to be declining, and prod ourselves with imaginary experiences of a highly erotic or lacerating character! Yet the law of gravity holds, and the longest flight ends in a descent, with a landing all the more bumpy for the exhaustion of the pilot.

Beyond the half-hour's silence lies a new beginning. Lawrence says: "Some old apocalyptist starts the second cycle—the death and regeneration of earth or world, instead of the individual." There are seven angels with seven trumpets. The Babylonian insistence upon the number *seven* is marked. We have it also in the *Book of Incantations.*

Four trumpets are blown—signals of destruction. (Lawrence points out the correspondence between the galloping of the four horsemen and the sounding of the four trumpets.) A third part of vegetable life, marine life, fresh-water life, and the energy of the heavens, is destroyed. Three "woes" announced by the remaining three of the seven angels follow. And now the action moves into the underworld of the cosmos, as in the first cycle it moved in the underworld of the self. The *abyss* is the place of the ancient, superseded powers of creation. The dethroned, fallen god becomes the demon, mischievous or malevolent. The degraded Apollo is Apollyon. In the day of Jewish Yahweh the most benevolent of Babylonian nature deities becomes a name for cursing. But never was there such a drive to the abyss as at the triumph of Christianity, when the sons of the morning became one and all tenants of hell. The abyss, however, is a "bottomless" pit. John of Patmos truthfully tells us that. The fears and taboos of Christianity can forge locks for the entrance to its dungeon, but the immortal prisoners will nevertheless escape. Osiris duly makes his voyage through the Underworld to reappear in the new dawn. Apollo is not missing from the Renaissance celebrations.

Brigit has only to make a slight change in her costume to be accepted as St. Bridget.

John of Patmos should be grateful to Lawrence for the latter's
ingenious interpretation of the first of the three "woes"—the locust army. But to me these composite bogeys of a Jewish malevolence, locusts like war-horses, with women's hair, men's faces,
lions' teeth, stings in their tails and the rest, are too badly constructed to be worth a couple of glances. Scarcely more convincing
are the two-hundred-thousand of dragonish creatures that issue
from nowhere in particular after the blowing of the sixth trumpet.
They are just Jewish-Christian images of fear and hatred towards
the Gentile and his god, just crude pictured curses. So I consign
them all to the nearest oblivion, and turn with more interest to
the figure which succeeds them on the Apocalyptic stage.

"A great cosmic lord," Lawrence calls him:

> *Clothed with a cloud, and a rainbow upon his head, and his face as
> it were the sun, and his feet as pillars of fire. And he had in his hand
> a little book open, and he set his right foot upon the sea and his left
> foot upon the earth, and cried with a loud voice as when a lion roareth;
> and when he had cried, seven thunders uttered their voices.*

The god-like being commands our attention:

> *And he lifted up his hand to heaven and sware by him that liveth
> for ever and ever, who created heaven, and the earth, and the sea, and
> the things that therein are, that there should be time no longer.*

Then, Lawrence says:

> . . . the seer is given the little book to eat. It is the lesser general or
> universal message of the destruction of the old world and creation of
> the new; a lesser message than that of the destruction of the old Adam
> and the creation of new man, which the seven-sealed book told.
> And it is sweet in the mouth, as revenge is sweet—but bitter in
> experience . . .

Sweet indeed must it have tasted in the mouth of the second-century Christian, passing from the flaming vision of his faith as it burned in his secret convocations, to the cold, contemptuous incomprehension of Roman society. And no less agreeable to every son of Adam, conscious that the burden and heat of the day are his, the leisure and fruit of it another's. A taste known to every leader of the people from Moses to Lenin.

XI

In Chapter XI the Temple is measured; it is difficult to see any reason or intention in the measuring. The two witnesses, the two olive-trees standing before Adonai, clothed in sackcloth, prophesy to the Gentiles.

These two witnesses Lawrence traces to the cult of the Twins, to Castor and Polydectes, and earlier Hellenic myth. They are the Dividers, those who hold asunder, the secret lords of sex, they are the "candlesticks"—"for they give the alternate forms of elemental consciousness, our day-consciousness and our night-consciousness."

Lawrence's interpretation is beautifully conceived and written —a fascinating study in symbolism. But I think it all has nothing to do with John of Patmos, who, having arrived at the Jewish Temple, is at home, with no immediate intention or necessity to excursion into Greek myth. I call to mind those two bronze-cased pillars, *Jachin* and *Boaz*, by tradition made of the wood of a tree planted by King David on Mount Zion, that stood at the entrance to Solomon's temple. Eliphaz Levi says of them:

These two pillars represented man and woman, reason and faith, power and liberty, Cain and Abel, right and duty. They were pillars of the intellectual and moral world, the monumental hieroglyphic of the antimony, inevitable to the grand law of creation.

If the pillars held for Jewish apocalyptists of the pre-Christian centuries the significance attributed to them by Levi, they were indeed witnesses for righteousness, suggestive enough to John's imagination. Their place will be before the heavenly temple in the new Jerusalem—that temple now declared open, because the reign of the King-God, the Sacrifice, is begun.

At this point in the text, says Lawrence, the older half of the *Apocalypse* ends.

XII

The second half begins in ancient Babylonia. We are back in the cities of the Euphrates long before King Hammurabi's day, long before Abram came from Ur of the Chaldees to establish his tribe in the Jordan Valley. The gods of greatest Babylon, Bel-Marduk and Ishtar, are yet unconceived. It is Dam-kina, the Earth-mother, whose fertility nourishes man. She bears and brings forth yearly, corn, fruit and flax—but how often are the crops devoured in their first freshness by the fierce sun, especially in the plateau region of the river's middle course! By the Sun-dragon, ever seeking to devour the Earth-mother's children.

And there appeared a great wonder in heaven; a woman clothed with the sun, and the moon under her feet, and upon her head a crown of twelve stars. And she, being with child, cried, travailing in birth, and pained to be delivered.

And there appeared another wonder in heaven; and behold a great red dragon, having seven heads and ten horns, and seven crowns upon his heads. And his tail drew the third part of the stars of heaven and did cast them to earth: and the dragon stood before the woman which was to be delivered, for to devour her child as soon as it was born.

So much of pure Babylonian myth. What follows is obviously of Jewish editing. The man-child of this birth is "to rule all nations with a rod of iron," he is "caught up unto God, and to his throne." While the woman finds sanctuary in a wilderness, where she is to be fed for 1,260 days—incidentally the same number given for the prophesying of the two "witnesses." We are back in the post-exilic Jewish world. A second jump brings us well into the Christian era. The sun-dragon becomes "that old serpent called the Devil and Satan, which deceiveth the whole world"— and the army of Jewish angels, commanded by Michael the Archangel, drives him down to the abyss.

In verse ten of this twelfth chapter we get an echo of the story of Job. And oh! what a jumble is the rest. Glorification of the Christian martyrs, who are said to have overcome the devil by "the blood of the Lamb." Commiseration for the "inhabiters of earth and sea" because the dragon-devil is so angry over his defeat that he is getting ready to wreak vengeance on mankind. The flight of the goddess on eagles' wings to the wilderness, and her pursuit by the dragon, who tries to drown her with a flood of water from his mouth—Earth swallows the flood, and the dragon turns to persecute the Christians, who are now "the remnant of her (the goddess's) seed which keep the commandments of God."

Lawrence thinks the myth of the Great Mother and the Dragon "the pivot of the *Apocalypse.*" He comments:

But . . . the goddess clothed with the sun and standing on the moon's crescent is difficult to reconcile with a Jewish vision. The Jews hated pagan gods, but they more than hated the great pagan goddesses; they would not even speak of them if possible. And this wonder-woman clothed in the sun and standing upon the crescent of the moon was too splendidly suggestive of the Magna Mater as she became to the Romans . . . How then does she come to tower as the central figure in a Jewish *Apocalypse?*

And his surmise is: "Religions of power must have a great queen and queen-mother. So here she stands in the *Apocalypse,* the book of thwarted power-worship."

But I cannot see any balanced significance in the inclusion of
the myth. Having been exiled to the wilderness she disappears
finally; there can be no place for her in the new Jerusalem, the
new heavens or the new earth. It may be, as Lawrence suggests,
that the pre-Christian Apocalyptist added her story to the original
pagan initiation manuscript, to express his vision of a Messiah's
birth. Or she may have been fitted into the *Book of Revelation* by
an editor of the third century, after the "Mother of God" cult had
developed within the Church. Such editing was probably obvious
to Jerome, who rejected the whole work, as did the scholars of the
Eastern Church.

Lawrence is loth to leave the Great Mother in banishment. I
see him glancing irritably through the next chapter, perhaps the
most original part of the book. He is not interested in the Nero-
Beast, and refuses to concern himself with any more large-scale
Christian destruction. But the Dragon catches his eye. The
Dragon, steering his mighty bulk through the ages, is a truly sig-
nifiicant figure.

In Höhlen wohnt der Drachen alte Brut—Queer that the caves
of the high Alps should have been the last retreat of the dispos-
sessed dragon of the Middle Ages. And yet, what fitter home
could Europe offer the creature of the heavens and the abyss?
Here comes Lawrence, a new Siegfried, to wake the hibernating
beast—not with the horn call of defiance, but with gentle, coaxing
speech—to lure him down, if it be possible, to levels of investi-
gation. Kindly, reassuring as L. is, I doubt if the dragon will
descend. I hardly expect to see them walking together below the
pines. I am afraid that the voice of Rhine-side factory-sirens will
prove more terrifying than the shout of Michael the Archangel.

Lawrence caresses the dragon. It is, he says, "the symbol of the
fluid, rippling, startling life within us." It is a potency

which can lie quite dormant, sleeping, and yet be ready to leap out
unexpectedly. Such are the sudden angers that spring upon us from

within ourselves . . . and the sudden accesses of violent desire, wild sexual desire, or violent hunger, or a desire of any sort, even for sleep.

It is this which surges in us to make us move, to make us act, to make us bring forth something; to make us spring up and live. Modern philosophers may call it *Libido* or *Elan Vital,* but the words are thin, they carry none of the wild suggestion of the dragon.

But it is necessary to make an ally of this beast.

Man can have the serpent with him or against him. When his serpent is with him, he is almost divine. When his serpent is against him, he is stung and envenomed and defeated from within. The great problem, in the past, was the conquest of the *inimical* serpent . . . the rousing of the splendid divine dragon within a man.

So there are really *two* dragons, two potencies, and one must subordinate the other. Or rather, this essential dragon of Lawrence's has two aspects, the benevolent and the malevolent. Woe betide you if the malevolent dragon gets on top!

When Moses set up the brazen serpent in the wilderness, an act which dominated the imagination of the Jews for many centuries, he was substituting the potency of the good dragon for the sting of the bad dragon, or serpents . . . What ails men to-day is that thousands of little serpents sting and envenom them all the time, and the great divine dragon is inert . . . He wakes on the lower planes of life; for a while in an airman like Lindbergh or a boxer like Dempsey. It is the little serpent of gold that lifts these two men for a brief time into a certain level of heroism. But on the higher planes there is no glimpse or gleam of the great dragon.

And there, D., you are wrong. You are like the Hebrew, stung by too many of the "thousands of little serpents" to be able to lift his eyes to the brazen gleam of the Great Serpent. Other men see him and live, other men seize upon his potency and feel its virtue rendering them immune against the poison of the stings. These men achieve; and you should know that achievement on the higher planes rarely takes spectacular form. You do know it, as certainly as that the golden fruit of the Pleiades still hangs on the tree of heaven, its sweet influences blessing the nights of the northern summer. But sometimes you forget, strangely, the essential things.

I love the way your imagination leaps after changing symbols like a kitten after a cord serpentining from my hand. Green beneficent dragon of the night, coiling among the stars, red maleficent dragon of the cosmos in its baleful aspect. Green dragon of the beginning of an era, beneficent, gradually changing to the red dragon of its end, malevolent.

The good potency of the beginning of the Christian era is now the evil potency of its end . . . This is a piece of very old wisdom and it will always be true. Time still moves in cycles, not in a straight line. And we are at the end of the Christian cycle. And the Logos, the good dragon of the beginning of the cycle, is the evil dragon of to-day. It will give its potency to no new thing, only to old and deadly things. It is the red dragon, and it must once more be slain by the heroes.

Lawrence *feels* this to be true, and his rotary-image way of thinking supplies him with the stuff of conviction. But here speaks L. Cranmer-Byng, who also has dragon-wisdom. "The Dragon-Spirit of Cosmic Change," says he, "was the symbol of the Taoist, the eternal growth which returns upon itself to produce new forms." And again, "Lung, the Dragon . . . is the embodiment of the Law of Becoming, and divine transmutation from new to old and old to new."[1]

What is the application of this with reference to the Christian era? The Word, being "made flesh," became subject to the natural law of mortality. Too much of mortality the Dragon-Logos took upon him, that he might "dwell among us." We "beheld his glory" and translated it in terms of materialism. We took the

[1] L. Cranmer-Byng, *The Vision of Asia* (London, John Murray, 1932).

gold of his shining scales and coined it, we wrought it into gold
of chalice and vestment and triple crown, we bound the souls of
men with fetters of its quality. And now the gold is lead to us.
The Dragon-Logos, whose body at the beginning of the era was
young and pliant, now sprawls in senile decay, and his weight is
an intolerable burden on the earth. Who shall rid us of the body
of this death? The heroes, Lawrence says. The heroes of this age
are those who shall slay this corrupting mass, this Word that was
made flesh, slay and burn it and dance round its pyre, whose
flames, high-darting, may direct them to the new sign of the immortal Dragon, hung out of heaven.

"What was a breath of inspiration becomes in the end a fixed
and evil form," says Lawrence. Then he digresses:

> Woman is more tightly coiled (in the folds of the old Logos) than
> man. To-day the best part of womanhood is wrapped tight and tense
> in the folds of the Logos, she is bodiless, abstract, and driven by a
> self-determination, terrible to behold. A strange "spiritual" creature is
> woman to-day, driven on and on by the evil demon of the old Logos,
> never for a moment allowed to escape and be herself.

This, and what follows about woman, is rather incoherent, to
me rather irritating. "Self-determination terrible to behold," is at
least as common in the man as in the woman of to-day. Wherever
it occurs, this tendency to say "I am a unit—I am a tight, compact,
self-sustained and self-sufficient organism," is evil, especially
when it is said consciously, by individual or nation. It impover-
ishes social life, it hampers economic life, impeding circulation
like a tightly-drawn ligature. Proclaimed by woman it is possibly
the more obviously undesirable, but man's voice reiterates this
declaration of egoism as insistently.

> The evil Logos says she (woman) must be "significant," she must
> make something worth while of her life. So on and on she goes,
> making something worth while, piling up the evil forms of our civili-

sation higher and higher, and never for a moment escaping to be wrapped in the brilliant fluid folds of the new green dragon.

D., I will tell you the reason why, in this matter of Woman, you make so many mistakes. It is because you fail to differentiate between the outward and apparent physical division of the sexes, and the *Yin* and *Yang*—the male and female principles that are the twin sources of life. You assume that the man—any man—is the unique human embodiment of the Yin, and the woman—any woman—is the unique human embodiment of the Yang. And this is not so. The male and female principles are not sundered completely and housed in separate bodies. They occur together, in the man and in the woman. There is more or less of the male principle in every man, more or less of the female principle in every woman; and as male and female flowers grow on each hazel bush, the complementary sex principles are present also in the human being. Some individuals embody the Yin and the Yang at balance or equipoise, or nearly so; these are the Whole Ones, complete in themselves, whose creative power can fertilise both men and women. In others, a much larger class, the male or the female predominates—these seek their complementary for purposes of creation, seek strenuously and blindly. Again, there are men and women in whom the two principles seem to fluctuate, alternately ruling the personality, which expresses itself capriciously, causing confusion.

When you, D., talk of Woman, your generalisations apply only to those women dominated by the Yang. You tend to perpetuate the old Semitic racial error symbolised in the story of the creation of Eve.

Nor can I agree with you that *all* our present life forms are evil. The contest between Good and Evil continues. There is still rhythm, there is still a (possibly unstable) balance between the opposing forces, the contending powers. Else we had arrived, not at the end of an era, but at the beginning of oblivion.

And our increasingly conscious effort, our attempt to make "something worth while" is not *necessarily* evil. It *may* become so if it is prolonged past its normal period. Our conscious corresponds with day in the world of phenomena, our unconscious with night. We cannot, without exhausting ourselves, without giving ourselves over to death, turn night into day. Alternating with the periods of a keenly-striving, strongly-willing conscious life, we ought to have, normally, periods of psychic sleep. Will and Intellect, twin-rulers of our To-day, must leave the throne to lords of the nearer and remoter past that continues its subdued existence within us. These Powers are not under our law, but know only the law of their own day, which to us is the anarchy of Dream. If we deny them the right of their immortality they become inimical to us; but acknowledged, their potency is the very foundation of our palace of achievement.

Lawrence returns to the dragons. The old red dragon of *Revelation,* he says, symbolised "the old form of power, kingship, riches, ostentation and lust." And this "foul dragon had to give way to the white dragon of the Logos—Europe with the glorification of white; the white dragon. It ends with the same sanitary worship of white, but the dragon is now a great white worm. Our colour is dirty-white or grey."

A worm! That was in Beowulf's day. The creature's last metamorphosis has a mulish aspect—or, seen in other light, it may resemble a half-submerged porpoise on which western deities make a proprietary tour round the world.

XIII

"We cannot," says Lawrence, "be very interested in the prophesied collapse of Rome and the Roman Empire." So by way of diversion he makes an examination of the dominant *numbers* of the *Apocalypse.*

Three. The "ancient threefold division of the living heavens, the Chaldean." The early Babylonian scheme of creation, symbolised by Anu, Bel, and Ea—sky, earth, and water. This echoed in the Jewish book of creation, *Genesis*, as the firmament or heaven, the dry land or earth, the gathering together of the waters, or seas. The perfect number of the Pythagoreans. Anaximander's *Boundless*, with its two elements, the hot and the cold, the dry and the moist, the fire and the dark, balanced on either side. The sacred number of the Christian Church, the number of the Trinity. Also, he might have noted, the sacred number of that older Egyptian Trinity, Osiris, Isis, and Horus. The simplest complete conception in plane geometry, the triangle. And the Persian mystic, D'Din Rumi, says that heaven has three times three spheres.

Four. Three is the number of things divine, and four is the number of creation. The world is four, four-square, divided into four quarters which are ruled by four great creatures, the four winged creatures that surround the throne of the Almighty. These four great creatures make up the sum of mighty space, both dark and light, and their wings are the quivering of this space, that trembles all the time with thunderous praise of the Creator: for these are Creation praising their Maker, as Creation shall praise its Maker forever.

I am tempted to quote at length here, to linger over finely-balanced and rhythmic passages. But since the reader will have, probably, Lawrence's book at hand, it is better only to remind him, by occasional phrase, of the beauty of its diction.

The living Cosmos was first divided into three parts, and then, at some point of great change, we cannot know when, man divided it instead into four quarters, and the four quarters demanded a whole, a conception of the whole, and then a maker, a Creator. So the four great elemental creatures became subordinate, they surrounded the supreme central unit, and their wings cover all space.

But by "a process of degradation" the concept of the Creatures

becomes, within the Christian church, the cherubim, the personi-
fied archangels, and finally the four evangelists.

Then we get the Four Elements of the Greeks, "the Big Four
of the Ages"—Earth, Air, Fire, Water.

When we consider the Four we shall see that they are, now and
forever, the four elements of our experience. All that science has
taught about fire does not make fire any different. The processes of
combustion are not fire, they are thought-forms. H_2O is not water, it
is a thought-form derived from experiments with water.

But D., the sense-perceived reality which I name *water* I may
also name H_2O. And H_2O is a fuller symbol than the word *water,*
because it conveys to me the past and future of the sense-perceived
reality, as well as its present.

Ah well! so would we argue in former days that project themselves vividly into the present. So, when this wrangle over *Revelation* is finished, we shall argue no more.

It is still fascinating, the matter of numbers. But to the Pythagoreans of the sixth century it was a divine mystery, and they its
priests. Nothing could be more sacred than their *tetractys,* the
wondrous triangle that combined the three of the heaven with
the four of the earth, and was thus the perfect symbol of the
cosmos.

And in the *Apocalypse,* says Lawrence, when John is referring
to the primal divine cosmos, he observes the three-fold division—
the dragon draws down a *third* of the stars with his tail, and so
on—but in the case of non-divine activities he uses the four-fold
division.

The sum of four and three, the divine and human, makes
seven—and the ubiquitous number necessarily haunts a work
dedicated to the seven churches of Asia. The Son of Man is seen
among the seven candlesticks, he holds seven stars in his right

hand. There are seven fiery lamps burning before the throne of
God. The immortal Lamb has seven horns and seven eyes. Then
we have the seven-sealed book, the seven angels of the "woes"
with their seven trumpets, the seven annunciatory thunders. But
it gets wearisome when seven *more* plague-bearing angels appear, and seven vials of wrath—and we can assume that the City
of the Seven Hills will be presented as the Scarlet Woman
mounted on the seven-headed beast.

Three, four, and seven are still the most significant of numbers.
By the fine, tenuous chain of unconscious memory they bind the
primitive to us and us to the primitive. We conceive them emotionally, not intellectually. On our calendar Sunday is the *first*
day of the week, but with the masses, the people of regular
rhythm, it is unconsciously regarded as the seventh, the week's
climax. There is an ending on Sunday night, a new beginning on
Monday morning. A child's seventh birthday is more important
than his sixth or eighth birthday—and at three times seven years
he becomes a full citizen. The Russians, trying to cut themselves
from their past, to live entirely on the level of present-day consciousness, are experimenting with a five-day week. They declare
the emotional bonds to be a tangle of dead bind-weed, choking
new life, and they would clear them all away as rubbish. Time
will either justify them, or show that short-sighted gardeners,
mistaking living roots for dead stems, can do much damage.

Seven is the number [says Lawrence] of the seven ancient planets,
which began with the sun and moon and included the five great
"wandering" stars, Jupiter, Venus, Mercury, Mars and Saturn. The
wandering planets were always a great mystery to man, especially in
the days when he lived breast to breast with the cosmos, and watched
the moving heavens with a profundity of attention quite different
from any form of attention to-day. . . . That the heaven-lore degener-
ated into tedious forms of divination and magic is only part of human

history: everything human degenerates, from religion downwards, and must be renewed and revived.

Has mankind ever lived "breast to breast with the cosmos?" If so, he was as unconscious of it as a day-old babe of its mother. It was before he learnt to say "I am Man!"

When I consider thy heavens, the work of thy fingers, the moon and the stars that thou hast ordained; what is man, that thou art mindful of him?

Aeons before, "the chief musician upon Gitteth" received that song from the king-bard. Detachment was then complete, and man had perceived great gulfs between the higher and lower planes of existence. The heavens had been scaled down to allow for the conception of a Creator above them; and mankind was the dwarfish recipient of a divine charity.

Our popular presentation of the cosmos draws man so large that the heavens and the Creator are small in comparison. Who shall show us the universe in beauty of proportion? When shall we be mature enough to perceive it "in the beauty of holiness"? For the power of seeing in *relative* proportion is an adult power, never present in the child; and mankind, being but adolescent, has not yet developed it in any marked or serviceable degree. Hitherto he has seen very partially and imperfectly, exaggerating, according to his age, the spiritual or the material aspects of what small vista of the cosmos his vision might command, and passing from one false scale of values to another. The process of degeneration of which Lawrence writes corresponds to the measure of a race's realisation of yet another failure, its gradual rejection of the scheme of philosophy based upon the last-conceived scale of values. Revulsion comes. Was *this* false?—then truth lies in its opposite. With child-like simplicity humanity reverses its scale of values, and is wrong again. The gods were not gods—they must be demons. It will be a great day when we realise that this process of reversal does not help us.

The old sacred number *seven*, losing its sanctity, became associated with the juggleries of magic, a fearful number. Rather in this connection, to heighten an atmosphere of fear, is it used in *Revelation*. *Ten*, the sacred *tetractys*, is only incidental, as the number of the horns both of the red dragon and the sea-beast. (These two horrific creatures are both crowned, but the former wears his crowns on his heads, the latter on his horns.) Old, widely-known symbols of power were the *horns*, as Lawrence points out—designating the direct, urgent force of the male, as in the bull Apis, but also the more subtle feminine force, as in horned Isis.

So we come to *twelve*. This number, says Lawrence,

> is the number of the established or unchanging cosmos. Twelve is the number of the signs of the zodiac, and of the months of the year. It is three times four or four times three: the complete correspondence. It is the whole round of heaven and the whole round of man.

His quiet tone of assertion changes; he satirises the confusion of symbolism and logic that characterised medieval theological disputation.

> For man has seven natures in the old scheme: that is 6 + 1, the last being the nature of his wholeness. But now he has another quite new nature, as well as the old one: for we admit that he is still made up of the old Adam plus the new. So now his number is twelve, 6 + 6 for his natures and one for his wholeness. But his wholeness is now in Christ; no longer symbolised between his brows. And now that his number is twelve, man is perfectly rounded and established, established and unchanging, for he is now perfect and there is no need for him to change, his wholeness, which is his thirteenth number, being with Christ in heaven. Such was the opinion of the "saved" concerning themselves. Such is still the orthodox opinion.

Well, well! there's a gospel of complacency.

But this triumphant dozen certainly marks the final victory of
the Jewish element in the *Apocalypse.* It was sacred to the Jews.
Twelve were the tribes, and twelve the stones on the high-priest's
breast-plate; so twice twelve became the number of the elders
seated about the throne in the Jewish-Christian heaven, and
twelve thousand the "elect" sealed from each tribe to be of the
Lamb's company. Their New Jerusalem upon its twelve founda-
tions would be entered by twelve gates, their Tree of Life bear
twelve fruits. The leaves of the Tree, we read, were for the healing of the nations; we may assume that the fruits would be strictly
a Jewish monopoly.

XIV

Lawrence gets very irritated over the concluding chapters, the
predominantly Jewish-Christian chapters of the *Apocalypse.*

When the great figures of mythology are turned into rationalised
or merely moral forces, then they lose interest. . . . What we have been
looking for in the *Apocalypse* is something older, grander than the
ethical business. The old flaming love of life and the strange shudder
of the presence of the invisible dead made the rhythm of really ancient
religion. Moral religion is comparatively modern, even with the Jews.

The association of *morality,* which is codified conduct, with *re-*
ligion, which is man's perception of his relationship to the cosmos,
seems at first sight curious. Examined closely their union is discovered to be a matter of convenience. While the human group
was co-conscious, entirely dominated by tribal-consciousness, its
cohesion was assured. No decalogue was necessary, the members
of the group submitted themselves in unquestioned obedience to
custom and taboo. But when individual consciousness appeared,
the group could only maintain its unity by building a wall of
morality against the intruder, by developing in its members a

sense of right and wrong. There had to be "thou shalts" and "thou shalt nots," with their related rewards and punishments: and thereafter the positive and negative *life* values, the qualities of good and evil, were applied to *acts*. A more or less clearly defined moral code appeared. Its "thou shalts" embodied the acts conducive to the maintenance of tribal unity, its "thou shalt nots" those prejudicial to solidarity. So we get, identified with the positive life values, the *good*, rightness, righteousness, complacency, reward; with the negative life values, the *evil*, wrong, guilt or sin, shame, and punishment. The Virtues and the Vices, crudely handsome or crudely hideous, were let loose in the world. And in the beginning of the struggle between the tribe and the newly-evolved individual, at the point where god-ideas were emerging, the latter were seized upon by the tribal consciousness and used as allies. Tribal sanctions were associated with the name of the tribal deity. This alliance between the tribe or group and its god enormously strengthened the group position. The Hebrew tribes produced an amazingly detailed code of sanctions and prohibitions, which were issued with the vehement *Thus saith Yahweh*.

The alliance still holds, and will as long as the popular conception of the anthropomorphic god is retained. But we see the individual consciousness, looking steadfastly upon Religion and Morality, declaring them to be neither one flesh nor one spirit. In Russia it has banished religion and humanised morality, but only by adopting the Ethic as god, and a material self-interest as the tribal cement. Here is no victory, but an armistice between the opposing forces of individuality and the tribe, upon terms far from favourable to the individual.

At the commencement of the Christian era the Church, deriving chiefly from Jewish sources, took over the Jewish deity and moral code, trimmed away such of the latter's provisions as had applied exclusively to Jewish national life, and used it as a halter whereby to control the young, vital, northern race that had trampled the Roman Empire. Western individuality suffered a bad reverse, and tribal consciousness became dominant for a thousand years and more.

And Lawrence is "acutely bored" by the Jewish moral angels and devils. He is no less acutely bored by the twentieth-century forms of this same old Jewish morality. We are again on a field of controversy well known to our youth.

The laws of life are made for the unseeing, unintelligent mass. But *entre nous,* and *entre nous* alone, we can make our own laws. Step out of the common pale and the old laws drop obsolete—and new laws suddenly reign.[2]

So, D., you asserted the right of the individual consciousness, and assumed the individual position at the beginning of your career. And here in the end of *Apocalypse* I find the conclusion to which you came after seventeen years of experiment. "To have an ideal for the individual which regards only his individual self and ignores his collective self is, in the long run, fatal."

To reconcile the conflicting ideals of the two selves is, however, virtually impossible. They are eternally antagonistic. One or the other must rule, one or the other be served.

"In us, one must rule, but the other be appeased," puts in D.

I hear a mocking voice, a tired voice, coming hollow through the distance. *Make to yourselves friends of the mammon of unrighteousness, that when ye fail, they may receive you to the everlasting habitations.*

In you, D., the individual self and the tribal self were so nearly matched that the contest between them was continuous and desperate. And now, weary of the struggle, you look longingly back through aeons of human development to days of co-consciousness, before strife began, when mankind was only sensible of "a flaming love of life and the strange shudder of the invisible dead."

---

[2] Letter to Helen Corke, 1911.

But for the European world that age was past long before the dawn of the Christian era. It will never come again for our race. You face to the past, I to the future, and neither knows whose in prospect is the longer journey—all that really matters is the next dawn, a day's strength, and sunset.

Let us finish with John of Patmos.

There is, then, the Beast with seven heads and ten horns, that rises from the sea—the Roman Empire, carrying the Scarlet Woman, Rome, who is drunken with the blood of Christian martyrs. There is the Dragon, become the Jewish symbol of evil, Satan. So much for Earth, and the Abyss. Up in heaven, the Jewish heaven of Mount Zion and the new Jerusalem, stands the Lamb with his 144,000 white-robed Jews, who are singing a hallelujah chorus, or appreciating an angelic recital of the horrors promised to the pagan Roman citizens, the fire and the brimstone, so that the smoke of their torment shall ascend for ever, and they have no rest day or night. There are pæans over the destruction of Rome and over the treading of the "wine-press of the wrath of God." Blood shall rise out of the wine-press "even to the horse bridles." The Reaper of this bloody harvest is to be "one like unto the Son of Man." A Jewish portrait of the philosopher who surrendered himself without protest to his political enemies, and healed by touch one slightly wounded by the most impetuous of his own followers.

Rome despatched, this Death Reaper deals generally with the Roman Empire, for "the beast and the kings of the earth and their armies gathered together to make war against him." He is, necessarily, victorious, and the "lake of fire that burneth with brimstone" receives the defeated. Then, as Lawrence says:

these precious martyrs all get their thrones, and for a thousand years the Lamb reigns over the earth, assisted by all the risen martyrs. And if the martyrs in the Millennium are going to be as bloodthirsty and ferocious as John the Divine in the *Apocalypse,* then somebody's going to get it hot during the rule of saints.

But this is not enough. After the thousand years the whole universe must be wiped out, earth, sun, moon, stars and sea . . . and a *new* New Jerusalem appear with the same old saints and martyrs in glory, and everything else should have disappeared except the lake of burning brimstone in which devils, demons, beasts and bad men shall fizzle and suffer for ever and ever. Amen!

"Surely," says Lawrence, "a rather repulsive work."

But who, during the last fourteen centuries, save Lawrence, and a few "advanced" theological writers, has regarded *Revelation* as a "work." It has been inspired mysticism, too sacred and dangerous to handle. The monk transcriber of the Middle Ages made his copy with extreme and anxious care, intimidated by the terrific curses at the book's end. Always, in time of religious persecution, it was the consolation of the agitated relatives and friends of those who suffered death. A high agony of love and pride and renunciation has fired its lyrical passages; branded them upon the Christian consciousness in the moments of its intensest experience. And for the masses to-day—for those incapable of intense experience, who feel at most a muddled half-ache of desolation and futility in the presence of death—there wakes an echo of vitality and beauty with the vague vision of the Blessed; not John's 144,000 sealed Jewish-Christian Blessed, but the day-to-day people hence departed, whose compensations for living were so few.

XV

Summing up his conclusions, Lawrence finds the *Book of Revelation* an expression of "the Christianity of the middling masses."
It is:

the feet of clay to the grand Christian image. . . . There is Jesus, but there is also John the Divine. There is Christian love—and there

is Christian envy. The former would "save" the world—the latter will
never finish till it has destroyed the world.

By the time of Jesus all the lowest classes and mediocre people had
realised that *never* would they get a chance to be kings, never would
they go in chariots, never would they drink wine from gold vessels.
Very well, then they would have their revenge by destroying it all.
"Babylon the Great is fallen, is fallen, and is become the habitation
of devils." How one hears the envy, the endless envy screeching
through this song of triumph.

I venture to suggest that if Lawrence had been able to revise his
writing here, he would have altered this passage. Such a realisation of class inferiority may occur from time to time; but it cannot be placed at any single point of history.

But the stuff of a religion—any religion—cannot be pure idealism. Religion (*religare*, to bind) must have its *binding* power.
Ideals are the flowers of the individual mind; when their seeds
germinate in other soil they absorb its different properties and the
new plants are modified accordingly. Or, to change the metaphor,
idealism, like a clear liquid, takes the shape and colour of the vessel into which it is poured. There would be no binding power in a
religion which could seed only in minds of the superior order, or
which shivered the flask of the commoner type of mind.

Now as long as the possessive instinct is strong and quick in
mankind, it will speak positively in terms of complacence and
negatively in terms of envy. Jesus, in whom it did not function,
warned his disciples against it. The Lord's Prayer ended originally
with the petition *"deliver us from evil."* But it would not do. The
lust of possession in ordinary mankind was too strong. The Kingdom, the Power, and the Glory had to come in. Then, said the
early Church, let the Kingdom, the Power, and the Glory be attributed to God—so shall there be no unseemly expression of desire in Christian prayer. Very good! By the time of St. Chrysostom
the addition was as much a part of the Lord's Prayer as it is now.

Thine is the Kingdom, the Power, and the Glory. But, said the Christians, we are Thine, and inheritors of the Kingdom, and so by and by it shall be *Ours.* The possessive instinct, recognised, is reinstated by the Church in both positive and negative forms. *To him that hath shall be given, and he shall have abundantly*—but also, conversely, *Blessed are the poor.* The medieval Most Christian kings follow naturally, and the equally Christian beggars whose feet the kings shall wash, once a year, in token of humility. But of course in the time of John of Patmos the possessive instinct of Christians could *only* speak in negative terms, those of envy, since the Church was poor and without honour in the world.

But Lawrence says that this fierce envy was the direct result of teaching the masses individual self-realisation.

Jesus gave the ideal for the Christian individual, and deliberately avoided giving one for the State or Nation. . . . Jesus saw the individual only, and considered only the individual. He left it to John of Patmos, who was up against the Roman State, to formulate the Christian vision of the Christian State. John did it in the *Apocalypse.* It entails the destruction of the whole world and the reign of saints in ultimate bodiless glory.

Because, as a matter of fact, when you start to teach individual self-realisation to the great masses of people, who, when all is said and done, are only *fragmentary* beings, *incapable* of whole individuality, you end by making them all envious, grudging, spiteful creatures. Anyone who is kind to men knows the fragmentariness of most men, and wants to arrange a society of power in which men fall naturally into a collective wholeness, since they *cannot* have an individual wholeness. In this collective wholeness they will be fulfilled. But if they make efforts at individual fulfillment they *must fail,* for they are by nature fragmentary. Then, failures, having no wholeness anywhere, they fall into envy and spite.

Now this was precisely the unconscious assumption of the Church which dominated the Middle Ages; the Church founded by the first-century Christians whose inhibited feelings of envy and revenge "screech" through the *Apocalypse*. And in essence the assumption was right. Men *are* more or less *whole* men, more or less capable of standing on two feet and looking up to heaven, of assuming the responsibility for their actions; they *are* bigger or smaller jets of vital force. Therefore the hierarchy is the natural arrangement of their society. If the Church had adopted this as a general principle, and made the *measure of wholeness* its criterion of the individual's position in the hierarchy, we might have been born in the kingdom of heaven as Jesus may have visualised it. But the Church could not do this. The real power of man, the full development of physical power and the glory of psychic vitality in freedom of thought and emotion were never given supreme place. Of these and their significance the Church lost sight, and confused *power* with *office,* and *glory* with *wealth*. As a consequence, in the City of God men did honour to mitre and crown, and brought their tribute to degenerate popes and bully kings. It was inevitable, this substitution of the trappings of royalty and priesthood for real kings and priests, because the Church derived its traditions chiefly from the degenerate Jewish priesthood and Roman State.

We must admit that the Church was prompt to recognise the occasional emergence of the hero, when his vitality was marked enough to make him the focus of a large tribal group. So it recognised Clovis, Pepin, Karl the Great, Olaf Tryggveson. To such men, whose lives would, anyhow, have been fulfilled in the measure of their own vital activities, the Church proffered the Jewish and Roman traditions of education, law, custom, the mellow fruit of civilisation. "All these things will I give thee if thou wilt worship Me," said the Church. And the bargain was struck. Similarly with the simpler baron. But the children and later descendants of these veritable leaders were not necessarily endowed with the qualities of leadership. They were frequently deficient in vitality, in wholeness, destitute of the qualities of individuality which had dominated their forefathers. Yet such native inferiority did not prevent them from inheriting, as a right, dignity of position, wealth, and the support of the Church. The hierarchy of the Middle Ages was therefore a false one, as insecure as a building planned without regard to the resolution of forces, with misplaced keystones and unbalanced strains and stresses. It was a hierarchy of this false kind that collapsed in Russia at the Revolution.

Lawrence says that the Millennium, the rule of the Martyrs, has come in Russia. "Strange, strange people they are, the martyrs, with weird, cold morality. When every country has its martyr-ruler, what a strange, unthinkable world it will be."

But this analogy can't be followed very far. Because the new "martyrs" want to distribute the soil's wealth, and the purple and fine linen—not to destroy it, as the old martyrs of the *Apocalypse* did. And the business of distribution is a much more difficult one than that of mere destruction—a fact which the whole economic world has recently realised. Even in its simplest form, the sharing of the material necessaries of life on a basis of equality, this distribution scheme would scarcely bring satisfaction, since the personal need is everywhere varied in both quantity and kind. And no one can apportion power, real living power; all that can be divided among the multitude is a dead authority.

XVI

A few vastly important points have been missed by Christian doctrine and Christian thought [observes Lawrence].

1. No man can be a pure individual. The mass of men have only the tiniest touch of individuality. The mass of men live and move, think and feel, collectively, and have practically no individual emotions or thoughts at all. They are fragments of the collective or social consciousness.

2. The State *cannot* have the psychology of an individual. Also it is a mistake to say that the State is made up of individuals. It is not. It is made up of a collection of fragmentary beings. And no collective act, even so private an act as voting, is made from the individual self.

Apropos of (1) it is noteworthy that at the present time individuality is becoming increasingly evident, to the disintegration of group consciousness. This individuality is not to be confused with *aristocracy*—it is merely a centrifugal force making for separation and "otherness." The aristocrat is inevitably an individual, but the individual is not necessarily an aristocrat.

Apropos of (2) it is important to remember that the "fragmentary beings" are each one *more* or *less* incomplete; and that in the present jumble of society no attempt is made to determine their true and relative position in the hierarchy.

3. The State *cannot* be Christian. Every State is a Power. It cannot be otherwise. Every State must guard its own boundaries and prosperity. If it fails to do so, it betrays all its individual citizens.

To "be Christian" may mean "to act according to the life principles formulated by Christ," or "to act in accordance with the dictates of the Church." The Church has systematically modified its requirements to meet the capacity of the adhering States, and in relation to it "Christian nations" have been many. But the philosophy of Christ, which includes the doctrine of non-aggression, non-resistance, and denial of the lust of possession, has never been accepted by a State. The collective consciousness has never admitted its practical possibility.

But a new ethic is now being evolved by the collective consciousness—a new morality to meet the recent change in the conditions of social permanence. The general disclosure of the secrets of scientific mass destruction threatens our race with annihilation. The State *cannot* at this stage, by any known offensive or defensive means, guard its own boundaries and prosperity. No State can protect its citizens from aerial bombardment, from the diffusion of poison gas, or from the loosed battalions of a deadly bacteria culture—the real weapons of war to-day. The danger is common to all States; the only safeguard against it is the achievement of a unity; the merging of the Many into the Whole.

4. Every citizen is a unit of worldly power. A man may wish to be a pure Christian and a pure individual. But since he *must* be a member of some political State or nation, he is forced to be a unit of worldly power.

Ignorance of this plain fact was the prime error of early Nonconformity, and *The Pilgrim's Progress* was its most vocal expression. Eighteenth- and nineteenth-century Nonconformity walled itself round with a crude individual arrogance uglier than the walls of its ugly chapels.

5. As a citizen, as a collective being, man has his fulfillment in the gratification of his power-sense. If he belongs to one of the so-called ruling nations his soul is fulfilled in the sense of his country's power or strength.

Not necessarily. It depends on the citizen's quota of individuality. If this be large, and he is in opposition to his country's use of its power, he may suffer humiliation on its account.

If his country mounts up aristocratically to a zenith of splendour and power, in a hierarchy, he will be all the more fulfilled, having his place in the hierarchy.

Assuredly, if such true hierarchy existed. But as yet it does not exist.

But if his country is powerful and democratic, then he will be obsessed with a perpetual will to assert his power in interfering and *preventing* other people from doing as they wish, since no man must do more than another man. . . . In democracy, bullying inevitably takes the place of power. Bullying is the negative form of power.

The bully is frequently the person who has been bullied, or whose natural power-sense has had no opportunity of release into action. But Lawrence uses the word *bullying* to mean "restraining from or hampering action, either by force or intimidation." In this sense it is truly the negative form of power, exercised by the usurper, the sham aristocrat, the jack-in-office.

> In a hierarchy each part is organic and vital, as my finger is an organic and vital part of me. But a democracy is bound in the end to be obscene, for it is composed of myriad disunited fragments, each fragment assuming to itself a false wholeness, a false individuality.

Again, this first statement would be true of a *real* hierarchy, but the kingdom of heaven is not come yet. As to present-day democracy, it would appear to be a political stage midway between —in terms of human progress—the false hierarchy and the true. It is an attempt at adjustment based on the false premise of man's "equality." How these "fragments" suffer to-day, from their sense of unfitness or of unused capacity, having no rest or satisfaction in themselves!

> 6. To have a creed of individuality which denies the reality of the hierarchy makes at last for anarchy. Democratic man lives by cohesion and resistance, the cohesive force of "love" and the resistant force of the individual "freedom." To yield entirely to love would be to be absorbed, which is the death of the individual, for the individual must hold his own or he ceases to be "free and individual."

The word "love" deflects Lawrence's mind from the consideration of the relation of the individual to the community. He returns, at the end of a long paragraph on its action in the purely personal relationship:

> What about the other love, "caritas," loving your neighbours as yourself? It works out the same. You love your neighbour. Immedi-

ately you run the risk of being absorbed by him: you must draw back,
you must hold your own. The love becomes resistance. In the end it is
all resistance and no love; which is the history of democracy.

No! D., it won't do. The individual love and the universal
love—charity—don't work out the same. You *cannot* love your
race or nation or religious community as you love the man or
woman who is dearest to you. The *universal* love is unreciprocal.
I love my nation. That is to say, I have a glowing sense of kin-
ship with its people, an abstract feeling unrelated to particular
persons; this feeling makes me desire to devote myself, my time
and energy and capabilities, more or less (according to the
strength of the feeling) to national service. And I do this, will-
ingly, because the *doing* of it contents and satisfies me. There
can be nothing reciprocal about this emotion—a community cannot love. As for loving one's neighbour—that is either a personal
matter or a piece of humbug—"I really ought to love my neighbour, so I will pretend I do"—that sort of thing, very common,
very irritating to the neighbour. The *individual* love, normal and
healthy, is reciprocal. One gives and one receives; this interchange
constitutes the joint creative act which may be consummated
physically, mentally, and spiritually, or all three (but this is rare).
The unhealthy form of individual love is a parasitism; in this
case there is no balance of exchange, but one of the two persons
gives little and demands much, to the exhaustion of the other. It
is evil, both natures are warped, and the creative purpose is
defeated.

Here D. turns on me with: "The individual cannot love. Let
that be an axiom!"

Very well! The utterly detached, fully self-conscious, complete
individual, isolate, more separate than Moon from Earth, eternally free to choose his own orbit, he cannot love. Completely
fulfilled in himself he will go down no more to the dark reservoir

of racial consciousness for renewal. He will neither call nor answer, and no union will draw from his vital substance for the creation of the Not He.

But there is no place in the Universe for such a being. And I think his entry into it might, like a grain of sand blown into a delicate mechanism, bring it to a standstill. In each of us more or less of individuality dwells, but there is no pure individual. We are still "all members of one body" and like to be.

The *Apocalypse,* strange book . . . shows the Christian in relation to the State, to the world and to the cosmos. It shows him in mad hostility to all of them, having, in the end, to will the destruction of them all.

It is the dark side of Christianity, of individualism and of democracy, the side the world at large now shows us. And it is, simply, suicide. Suicide individual and *en masse.* If man could will it, it would be cosmic suicide. But the cosmos is not at man's mercy, and the sun will not perish to please us.

(D., you are forcing the analogy beyond its natural limit. You are projecting your own shadow over humanity.)

We are unnaturally resisting our connection with the cosmos, with the world, with mankind, with the nation, with the family. All these connections are, in the *Apocalypse,* anathema to us. We cannot bear connection. That is our malady. We must break away, and be isolate. Beyond a certain point, which we have reached, it is suicide. Perhaps we have chosen suicide.

The passage changes into the singular as I read it.

But the *Apocalypse* shows, by its very resistance, the things that the human heart secretly yearns after. . . . What man most passionately wants is his living wholeness and his living unison, not his own isolate salvation of his "soul." Man wants his physical fulfilment first and foremost, since now, once and once only, he is in the flesh, and potent. For man the vast marvel is to be alive. For man, as for flower and beast and bird, the supreme triumph is to be most vividly, most perfectly alive. Whatever the unborn and the dead may know, they cannot know the beauty, the marvel of being alive in the flesh.

That is the lesson David taught twenty years ago, passionately and persistently, to one who would hardly be persuaded, who had conceived her function only as a despairing service in the temple of Isis-in-Search. The same lesson, but now it is Lawrence speaking—Lawrence, whose body is wasting to death before his undimmed eyes, for whom that "supreme triumph" is already the memory of past and irrecoverable experience. There is nothing in our language more wistful.

The magnificent here and now of life in the flesh is ours, and ours alone, and ours only for a time. We ought to dance with rapture that we should be alive and in the flesh, and part of the living incarnate cosmos.

It is a good thing to tell a generation overmuch concerned about its growing-pains. A good message with which to leave it. For Lawrence, the initiate, passes on:

> Give me the moon at my feet,
>   Put my feet upon the crescent, like a Lord!
> O, let my ankles be bathed in moonlight that
>   I may go
>   sure and moonshod, cool and bright-footed
> Towards my goal—
>
> Reach me a gentian, give me a torch!
> let me guide myself with the blue-forked
>   torch of this flower
>   down the darker and darker stairs, where
>   blue is darkened on blueness
>   even where Persephone goes—[3]

---

[3] *Last Poems* (Florence, Orioli, 1932).

He has put off the garments of flesh, the four physical natures; as he descends I hear his diminishing voice repeating a new lesson:

> My soul knows that I am part of the human race,
>   My soul is an organic part of the great
>   human soul.
> The mind has no existence by itself,
>   it is only the sun-glitter on the surface
>   of the waters.
>   My individualism is an illusion. . . .
>   I am a part of the great whole. . . .

INDEX

Abram: 104

Addington, England: 61, 77

Adonai: 103

Alcestis: 8

allegory: Revelation as, 62–63, 64; Helen Corke on, 64–65; Lawrence on, 64–65

Annesley (in "Nethermere"): 50

Anaximander: 112

Apis: 116

Apocalypse. See REVELATION, BOOK OF

Apocalypse (Lawrence's): Jessie Chambers' interest in, 40. SEE ALSO *Lawrence and* APOCALYPSE; Lawrence, D. H., on *Revelation*

apocalyptist: Jewish, in writing REVELATION, 86, 89, 101, 104, 106; Jewish-Christian, in writing REVELATION, 86, 89, 102. SEE ALSO John of Patmos

Apollo: 101

Appollyon: 101

Apostle's Creed: initiation ritual in, 99

aristocracy. SEE Corke, Helen, philosophy of; Lawrence, D. H. philosophy of

Arnold, England: 24

Arno Vale (farm): as Jessie Chambers' home, 24; Helen Corke visits, 25, 26–27, 29–30

Anu: 112

Artemis: 89

Arthur (in "Nethermere"): 54

Assyria: friezes of, 90; mentioned, 88

astrology: symbolism of, in REVELATION, 114, 116

Ave Atque Vale: 9

Babylonia: initiation ritual of, 98–99; significance of seven in, 101; myth of, in REVELATION, 104; scheme of creation of, 112; mentioned, 88

Bach, Johann Sebastian: 97

Beethoven, Ludwig von: 3

Bel: 112

Bel-Marduk: 88, 104

Beowulf: 111

Boaz (pillar): 103

Bordeaux, France: Jessie visits, 36, 37

Bournemonth, England: 31